ABOUT THIS PUBLICATION

FOR SERVICE ASSISTANCE

Customer Service Department
704.898.0770

North Carolina General Statues is published by The Muliti-Media Group of Greater Charlotte in Charlotte, North Carolina.

The records required by U.S. Code 2257(a) through (c) and the pertinent regulations 28 C.F.R. Cli. 1, Part 75 with respect to this publication and all materials associated with such records are maintained by The Multi-Media Group of Greater Charlotte, Publisher and available for review by Attorney General.

www.visionbooks.org

TID: 4993176
ISBN (10) digit: 1502331217
ISBN (13) digit: 978-1502331212

123-4-56789-01234-Paperback
123-4-56789-01234-Hardback

First Edition

090520140547

Printed in the United States of America

1

2015 EDITION

North Carolina Criminal Law

And Procedure-Pamphlet # 11

Printed In conjunction with the

Administration of the Courts

North Carolina Criminal Law and Procedure
Pamphlet Reference Guide

8

9

10

11

12

13

14

§ 15A-1368.5. Commencement of post-release supervision; multiple sentences.

A period of post-release supervision begins on the day the prisoner is released from imprisonment. Periods of post-release supervision run concurrently with any federal or State prison, jail, probation, or parole terms to which the prisoner is subject during the period, only if the jurisdiction which sentenced the prisoner to prison, jail, probation, or parole permits concurrent crediting of supervision time. (1993, c. 538, s. 20.1; 1994, Ex. Sess., c. 24, s. 14(b).)

§ 15A-1368.6. Arrest and hearing on post-release supervision violation.

(a)   Arrest for Violation of Post-Release Supervision. - A supervisee is subject to arrest by a law enforcement officer or a post-release supervision officer for violation of conditions of post-release supervision only upon issuance of an order of temporary or conditional revocation of post-release supervision by the Commission. However, a post-release supervision revocation hearing under subsection (e) of this section may be held without first arresting the supervisee.

(b)   When and Where Preliminary Hearing on Post-Release Supervision Violation Required. - Unless the hearing required by subsection (e) of this section is first held or a continuance is requested by the supervisee, a preliminary hearing on supervision violation shall be held reasonably near the place of the alleged violation or arrest and within seven working days of the arrest of a supervisee to determine whether there is probable cause to believe that the supervisee violated a condition of post-release supervision. Otherwise, the supervisee shall be released seven working days after arrest to continue on supervision pending a hearing. If the supervisee is not within the State, the preliminary hearing is as prescribed by G.S. 148-65.1A.

(b1)   Bail Following Arrest for Violation of Post-Release Supervision if Releasee Is a Sex Offender. - Notwithstanding subsection (b) of this section, if the releasee has been convicted of an offense that requires registration under Article 27A of Chapter 14 of the General Statutes and is arrested for a violation in accordance with this section, the releasee shall be detained without bond until the preliminary hearing is conducted.

(c)   Officers to Conduct Preliminary Hearing. - The preliminary hearing on post-release supervision violation shall be conducted by a judicial official, or by a hearing officer designated by the Commission. A person employed by the

Division of Adult Correction of the Department of Public Safety shall not serve as a hearing officer at a hearing provided by this section unless that person is a member of the Commission, or is employed solely as a hearing officer.

(d)   Procedure for Preliminary Hearing. - The Division of Adult Correction of the Department of Public Safety shall give the supervisee notice of the preliminary hearing and its purpose, including a statement of the violations alleged. At the hearing, the supervisee may appear and speak in the supervisee's own behalf, may present relevant information, and may, on request, personally question witnesses and adverse informants, unless the hearing officer finds good cause for not allowing confrontation. If the person holding the hearing determines there is probable cause to believe the supervisee violated conditions of supervision, the hearing officer shall summarize the reasons for the determination and the evidence relied on. Formal rules of evidence do not apply at the hearing. If probable cause is found, the supervisee may be held in the custody of the Division of Adult Correction of the Department of Public Safety to serve the appropriate term of imprisonment, subject to the outcome of a revocation hearing under subsection (e) of this section.

(e)   Revocation Hearing. - Before finally revoking post-release supervision, the Commission shall, unless the supervisee waived the hearing or the time limit, provide a hearing within 45 days of the supervisee's reconfinement to determine whether to revoke supervision finally. For purposes of this subsection, the 45-day period begins when the preliminary hearing required by subsection (b) of this section is held or waived, or upon the passage of seven working days after arrest, whichever is sooner. The Commission shall adopt rules governing the hearing. (1993, c. 538, s. 20.1; 1994, Ex. Sess., c. 24, s. 14(b); 1996, 2nd Ex. Sess., c. 18, s. 20.15(b); 1997-237, s. 1; 2000-189, s. 1; 2008-117, s. 20; 2011-145, s. 19.1(h).)

Article 84B.

Medical Release of Inmates.

§ 15A-1369. Definitions.

16

For purposes of this Article, the term:

(1)   "Commission" means the Post-Release Supervision and Parole Commission.

(2)   "Division" means the Division of Adult Correction of the Department of Public Safety.

(3)   "Geriatric" describes an inmate who is 65 years of age or older and suffers from chronic infirmity, illness, or disease related to aging that has progressed such that the inmate is incapacitated to the extent that he or she does not pose a public safety risk.

(4)   "Inmate" means any person sentenced to the custody of the Division of Adult Correction of the Department of Public Safety.

(5)   "Medical release" means a program enabling the Commission to release inmates who are permanently and totally disabled, terminally ill, or geriatric.

(6)   "Medical release plan" means a comprehensive written medical and psychosocial care plan that is specific to the inmate and includes, at a minimum:

a.   The proposed course of treatment;

b.   The proposed site for treatment and post-treatment care;

c.   Documentation that medical providers qualified to provide the medical services identified in the medical release plan are prepared to provide those services; and

d.   The financial program in place to cover the cost of this plan for the duration of the medical release, which shall include eligibility for enrollment in commercial insurance, Medicare, or Medicaid or access to other adequate financial resources for the duration of the medical release.

(7)   "Permanently and totally disabled" describes an inmate who, as determined by a licensed physician, suffers from permanent and irreversible physical incapacitation as a result of an existing physical or medical condition that was unknown at the time of sentencing or, since the time of sentencing, has progressed to render the inmate permanently and totally disabled, such that the inmate does not pose a public safety risk.

(8)   "Terminally ill" describes an inmate who, as determined by a licensed physician, has an incurable condition caused by illness or disease that was unknown at the time of sentencing or, since the time of sentencing, has progressed to render the inmate terminally ill, and that will likely produce death within six months, and that is so debilitating such that the inmate does not pose a public safety risk. (2008-2, s. 1; 2011-145, s. 19.1(h).)

§ 15A-1369.1. Authority to release.

The Commission shall establish a medical release program to be administered by the Department. The Commission shall prescribe when and under what conditions an inmate may be released for medical release, consistent with the provisions of G.S. 15A-1369.4. The Commission may adopt rules to implement the medical release program. (2008-2, s. 1.)

§ 15A-1369.2. Eligibility.

(a)   Except as otherwise provided in this section, notwithstanding any other provision of law, an inmate is eligible to be considered for medical release if the Department determines that the inmate is:

(1)   Diagnosed as permanently and totally disabled, terminally ill, or geriatric under the procedure described in G.S. 15A-1369.3(b)(1); and

(2)   Incapacitated to the extent that the inmate does not pose a public safety risk.

(b)   Persons convicted of a capital felony or a Class A, B1, or B2 felony and persons convicted of an offense that requires registration under Article 27A of Chapter 14 of the General Statutes shall not be eligible for release under this Article. (2008-2, s. 1.)

§ 15A-1369.3. Procedure for medical release.

18

(a)   The Commission shall consider an inmate for medical release upon referral by the Department. The Department may base its referral upon either a request or petition for release filed by the inmate, the inmate's attorney, or the inmate's next of kin or upon a recommendation from within the Department.

(b)   The referral shall include an assessment of the inmate's medical and psychosocial condition and the risk the inmate poses to society, as follows:

(1)   The Department medical director, or a designee of the director who is a licensed physician, shall review the case of each inmate who meets the eligibility requirements for medical release set forth in G.S. 15A-1369.2. Any physician who examines an inmate being considered for medical release shall prepare a written diagnosis that includes:

a.   A description of any and all terminal conditions, physical incapacities, and chronic conditions; and

b.   A prognosis concerning the likelihood of recovery from any and all terminal conditions, physical incapacities, and chronic conditions.

(2)   The Department shall make an assessment of the risk for violence and recidivism that the inmate poses to society. In order to make this assessment, the Department may consider such factors as the inmate's medical condition, the severity of the offense for which the inmate is incarcerated, the inmate's prison record, and the release plan.

(c)   If the Department determines that the inmate meets the criteria for release, the Department shall forward its referral and medical release plan for the inmate to the Commission. The Department shall complete the risk assessment and forward its referral and medical release plan within 45 days of receiving a request, petition, or recommendation for release.

(d)   The Commission shall make a determination of whether to grant medical release within 15 days of receiving a referral from the Department for release of a terminally ill inmate and within 20 days of receiving a referral from the Department for release of a permanently and totally disabled inmate or a geriatric inmate. In making the determination, the Commission shall make an independent assessment of the risk for violence and recidivism that the inmate poses to society. The Commission also shall provide the victim or victims of the inmate or the victims' family or families with an opportunity to be heard.

(e)   A denial of medical release by the Commission shall not affect an inmate's eligibility for any other form of parole or release under applicable law.

(f)   If the Department determines that an inmate should not be considered for release under this Article or the Commission denies medical release under this Article, the inmate may not reapply or be reconsidered unless there is a demonstrated change in the inmate's medical condition. (2008-2, s. 1.)

§ 15A-1369.4. Conditions of medical release.

(a)   The Commission shall set reasonable conditions upon an inmate's medical release that shall apply through the date upon which the inmate's sentence would have expired. These conditions shall include:

(1)   That the released inmate's care be consistent with the care specified in the medical release plan as approved by the Commission;

(2)   That the released inmate shall cooperate with and comply with the prescribed medical release plan and with reasonable requirements of medical providers to whom the released inmate is to be referred to continued treatment;

(3)   That the released inmate shall be subject to supervision by the Section of Community Corrections of the Division of Adult Correction and shall permit officers from the Division to visit the inmate at reasonable times at the inmate's home or elsewhere;

(4)   That the released inmate shall comply with any conditions of release set by the Commission; and

(5)   That the Commission shall receive periodic assessments from the inmate's treating physician.

(b)   The Commission shall promptly order an inmate returned to the custody of the Division to await a revocation hearing if the Commission receives credible information that an inmate has failed to comply with any reasonable condition set upon the inmate's release. If the Commission subsequently revokes an inmate's medical release for failure to comply with conditions of release, the inmate shall resume serving the balance of the sentence with credit given only for the duration of the inmate's medical release served in compliance with all reasonable conditions set forth pursuant to subsection (a) of this section. Revocation of an inmate's medical release for violating a condition of release shall not preclude an inmate's eligibility for any other form of parole or release provided by law but may be used as a factor in determining eligibility for that parole or release. (2008-2, s. 1; 2011-145, s. 19.1(h), (k).)

§ 15A-1369.5. Change in medical status.

(a)   If a periodic medical assessment reveals that an inmate released on medical release has improved so that the inmate would not be eligible for medical release if being considered at that time, the Commission shall order the inmate returned to the custody of the Department to await a revocation hearing. In determining whether to revoke medical release, the Commission shall consider the most recent medical assessment of the inmate and a risk assessment of the inmate conducted pursuant to G.S. 15A-1369.3(b)(2). If the Commission revokes the inmate's medical release, the inmate shall resume serving the balance of the sentence with credit given for the duration of the medical release.

(b)   Revocation of an inmate's medical release due to a change in the inmate's medical condition shall not preclude an inmate's eligibility for medical release in the future or for any other form of parole or release provided by law. (2008-2, s. 1.)

§ 15A-1370. Reserved for future codification purposes.

Article 85.

Parole.

§ 15A-1370.1. Applicability of Article 85.

This Article is applicable to all prisoners serving sentences of imprisonment for convictions of impaired driving under G.S. 20-138.1. This Article does not apply to a prisoner serving a sentence of life imprisonment without parole. A prisoner serving a sentence of life imprisonment without parole shall not be eligible for parole at any time. (1979, c. 760, s. 4; 1979, 2nd Sess., c. 1316, s. 41; 1981, c. 662, s. 3; 1993, c. 538, s. 21; 1994, Ex. Sess., c. 21, s. 2, c. 22, ss. 33, 34, c. 24, s. 14(b).)

§ 15A-1371. Parole eligibility, consideration, and refusal.

(a)   Eligibility. - Unless his sentence includes a minimum sentence, a prisoner serving a term of imprisonment for a conviction of impaired driving under G.S. 20-138.1 other than one included in a sentence of special probation imposed under authority of this Subchapter is eligible for release on parole at any time. A prisoner whose sentence includes a minimum term of imprisonment imposed under authority of this Subchapter is eligible for release on parole only upon completion of the service of that minimum term or one fifth of the maximum penalty allowed by law for the offense for which the prisoner is sentenced, whichever is less, less any credit allowed under G.S. 15A-1355(c) and Article 19A of Chapter 15 of the General Statutes. A prisoner sentenced under the Fair Sentencing Act for a Class D through Class J felony, who meets the criteria established pursuant to this section, is eligible for parole consideration after completion of the service of at least 20 years imprisonment less any credit allowed under applicable State law.

(a1)   Repealed by Session Laws 1994, Ex. Sess., c. 21, s. 3.

(b)   (1),   (2) Repealed by Session Laws 1993, c. 538, s. 22.

(3)   Whenever the Post-Release Supervision and Parole Commission will be considering for parole a prisoner serving a sentence of life imprisonment the Commission must notify, at least 30 days in advance of considering the parole, by first class mail at the last known address:

a.   The prisoner;

b.   The district attorney of the district where the prisoner was convicted;

c.   The head of the law enforcement agency that arrested the prisoner and the sheriff of the county where the crime occurred;

22

d.   Any of the victim's immediate family members who have requested in writing to be notified; and

e.   Repealed by Session Laws 1993, c. 538, s. 22.

f.   As many newspapers of general circulation and other media in the county where the defendant was convicted and if different, in the county where the prisoner was charged, as reasonable. The Commission may elect to use electronic means rather than the mail to notify the media under this sub-subdivision if such notification would be more timely and cost-effective.

The Post-Release Supervision and Parole Commission must consider any information provided by any such parties before consideration of parole. The Commission must also give the district attorney, the head of the law enforcement agency who has requested in writing to be notified, the victim, any member of the victim's immediate family who has requested to be notified, and as many newspapers of general circulation and other media in the county or counties designated in sub-subdivision f. of this section as reasonable, written notice of its decision within 10 days of that decision. The Commission may elect to use electronic means rather than the mail to notify the media under this paragraph if such notification would be more timely and cost-effective. The Parole Commission shall not, however, include the name of any victim in its notification to the newspapers and other media.

(c)   Repealed by Session Laws 1993, c. 538, s. 22.

(d)   Criteria. - The Post-Release Supervision and Parole Commission may refuse to release on parole a prisoner it is considering for parole if it believes:

(1)   There is a substantial risk that he will not conform to reasonable conditions of parole; or

(2)   His release at that time would unduly depreciate the seriousness of his crime or promote disrespect for law; or

(3)   His continued correctional treatment, medical care, or vocational or other training in the institution will substantially enhance his capacity to lead a law-abiding life if he is released at a later date; or

(4)   There is a substantial risk that he would engage in further criminal conduct.

(e)   Refusal of Parole. - A prisoner who has been granted parole may elect to refuse parole and to serve the remainder of his term of imprisonment.

(f)   Repealed by Session Laws 1993, c. 538, s. 22.

(g)   Notwithstanding the provisions of subsection (a), a prisoner serving a sentence of not less than 30 days nor as great as 18 months for impaired driving may be released on parole when he completes service of one-third of his maximum sentence unless the Post-Release Supervision and Parole Commission finds in writing that:

(1)   There is a substantial risk that he will not conform to reasonable conditions of parole; or

(2)   His release at that time would unduly depreciate the seriousness of his crime or promote disrespect for law; or

(3)   His continued correctional treatment, medical care, or vocational or other training in the institution will substantially enhance his capacity to lead a law-abiding life if he is released at a later date; or

(4)   There is a substantial risk that he would engage in further criminal conduct.

If a prisoner is released on parole by operation of this subsection, the term of parole is the unserved portion of the sentence to imprisonment, and the conditions of parole, unless otherwise specified by the Post-Release Supervision and Parole Commission, are those authorized in G.S. 15A-1374(b)(4) through (10).

In order that the Post-Release Supervision and Parole Commission may have an adequate opportunity to make a determination whether parole under this section should be denied, no prisoner eligible for parole under this subsection shall be released from confinement prior to the fifth full working day after he shall have been placed in the custody of the Secretary of Public Safety or the custodian of a local confinement facility.

(h)   Community Service Parole. - Notwithstanding the provisions of any other subsection herein, prisoners serving sentences for impaired driving shall be eligible for community service parole after serving the minimum sentence required by G.S. 20-179, in the discretion of the Post-Release Supervision and Parole Commission.

Community service parole is early parole for the purpose of participation in community service under the supervision of the Section of Community Corrections of the Division of Adult Correction. A parolee who is paroled under this subsection must perform as a condition of parole community service in an amount and over a period of time to be determined by the Post-Release Supervision and Parole Commission. However, the total amount of community service shall not exceed an amount equal to 32 hours for each month of active service remaining in his minimum sentence. The Post-Release Supervision and Parole Commission may grant early parole under this section without requiring the performance of community service if it determines that such performance is inappropriate to a particular case.

The probation/parole officer and the judicial services coordinator shall develop a program of community service for the parolee. The coordinator shall report any willful failure to perform community service work to the probation/parole officer. Parole may be revoked for any parolee who willfully fails to perform community service work as directed by the Section of Community Corrections of the Division of Adult Correction. The provisions of G.S. 15A-1376 shall apply to this violation of a condition of parole.

Community service parole eligibility shall be available to a prisoner:

(1)   Who is serving an active sentence the term of which exceeds six months; and

(2)   Who, in the opinion of the Post-Release Supervision and Parole Commission, is unlikely to engage in further criminal conduct; and

(3)   Who agrees to complete service of his sentence as herein specified; and

(4)   Who has served one-half of his minimum sentence, at least 10 days if sentenced to Level One punishment or at least seven days if sentenced to Level Two punishment, whichever is longer.

In computing the service requirements of subdivision (4) of this subsection, credit shall be given for good time and gain time credit earned pursuant to G.S. 148-13 but only after a person has served at least 10 days if sentenced to Level

25

One punishment or at least seven days if sentenced to Level Two punishment. Nothing herein is intended to create or shall be construed to create a right or entitlement to community service parole in any prisoner.

(i)   The fee required by G.S. 143B-708 shall be paid by all persons who participate in the Community Service Parole Program.

(j)   The Post-Release Supervision and Parole Commission may terminate a prisoner's community service parole before the expiration of the term of imprisonment where doing so will not endanger the public, unduly depreciate the seriousness of the crime, or promote disrespect for the law. (1977, c. 711, s. 1; 1977, 2nd Sess., c. 1147, ss. 19A-22; 1979, c. 749, ss. 9, 10; 1979, 2nd Sess., c. 1316, s. 42; 1981, c. 63, s. 1; c. 179, s. 14; 1983 (Reg. Sess., 1984), c. 1098, s. 1; 1985, c. 453, ss. 1, 2; 1985 (Reg. Sess., 1986), c. 960, s. 2; c. 1012, ss. 2, 5; 1987, c. 47; c. 783, s. 7; 1989, c. 1, ss. 3, 4; 1991, c. 217, s. 3; c. 288, s. 2; 1993, c. 538, s. 22; 1994, Ex. Sess., c. 21, s. 3; c. 24, s. 14(b); c. 25, ss. 1, 2; 2002-126, s. 29A.1(a); 2006-264, s. 34; 2008-133, s. 1; 2009-372, s. 13(a), (b); 2009-451, s. 19.26(a), (d); 2009-575, s. 16A; 2010-107, s. 1; 2011-145, s. 19.1(i), (k); 2013-348, s. 3; 2013-368, s. 20.)

§ 15A-1372. Length and effect of parole term.

(a)   Term of Parole. - The term of parole for any person released from imprisonment may be no greater than one year.

(b)   Repealed by Session Laws 1993, c. 538, s. 23, effective October 1, 1994.

(c)   Termination of Sentence. - When a parolee completes his period of parole, the sentence or sentences from which he was paroled are terminated.

(d)   Repealed by Session Laws 1993, c. 538, s. 23, effective October 1, 1994. (1977, c. 711, s. 1; 1981, c. 642; 1989, c. 1, s. 8; 1989 (Reg. Sess., 1990), c. 1031, s. 3; 1991, c. 217, s. 1; 1993, c. 538, s. 23; 1994, Ex. Sess., c. 21, s. 4, c. 24, s. 14(b).)

§ 15A-1373. Incidents of parole.

(a)   Conditionality of Parole. - Unless terminated sooner as provided in subsection (b), parole remains conditional and subject to revocation.

(b)   Early Termination. - The Post-Release Supervision and Parole Commission may terminate a period of parole and discharge the parolee at any time after the expiration of one year of successful parole if warranted by the conduct of the parolee and the ends of justice.

(c)   Modification of Conditions. - The Post-Release Supervision and Parole Commission may for good cause shown modify the conditions of parole at any time prior to the expiration or termination of the period for which the parole remains conditional.

(d)   Effect of Violation. - If the parolee violates a condition at any time prior to the expiration or termination of the period, the Commission may continue him on the existing parole, with or without modifying the conditions, or, if continuation or modification is not appropriate, may revoke the parole as provided in G.S. 15A-1376 and reimprison the parolee for a term consistent with the following requirements:

(1)   The time the parolee was at liberty on parole and in compliance with all terms and conditions of that parole shall be credited on a day-for-day basis against the maximum term of imprisonment imposed by the court under G.S. 15A-1351, except that the parolee shall receive no credit for the last six months of his parole.

(2)   The prisoner must be given credit against the term of reimprisonment for all time spent in custody as a result of revocation proceedings under G.S. 15A-1376.

(e)   Re-parole. - A prisoner who has been reimprisoned following parole may be re-paroled by the Post-Release Supervision and Parole Commission subject to the provisions which govern initial parole. In the event that a defendant serves the final six months of his maximum imprisonment as a result of being recommitted for violation of parole, he may not be required to serve a further period on parole.

(f)   Timing of Revocation. - The Post-Release Supervision and Parole Commission may revoke parole for violation of a condition during the period of parole. The Commission also may revoke following the period of parole if:

(1)   Before the expiration of the period of parole, the Commission has recorded its intent to conduct a revocation hearing, and

(2)   The Commission finds that every reasonable effort has been made to notify the parolee and conduct the hearing earlier. (1977, c. 711, s. 1; 1979, c. 927; 1991, c. 217, s. 2; 1993, c. 538, s. 38; 1994, Ex. Sess., c. 24, s. 14(b).)

§ 15A-1374. Conditions of parole.

(a)   In General. - The Post-Release Supervision and Parole Commission may in its discretion impose conditions of parole it believes reasonably necessary to insure that the parolee will lead a law-abiding life or to assist him to do so. The Commission must provide as an express condition of every parole that the parolee not commit another crime during the period for which the parole remains subject to revocation. When the Commission releases a person on parole, it must give him a written statement of the conditions on which he is being released.

(a1)   Required Conditions for Certain Offenders. - A person serving a term of imprisonment for an impaired driving offense sentenced pursuant to G.S. 20-179 that:

(1)   Has completed any recommended treatment or training program required by G.S. 20-179(p)(3); and

(2)   Is not being paroled to a residential treatment program;

shall, as a condition of parole, receive community service parole pursuant to G.S. 15A-1371(h), or be required to comply with subdivision (b)(8a) of this section.

(b)   Appropriate Conditions. - As conditions of parole, the Commission may require that the parolee comply with one or more of the following conditions:

(1)   Work faithfully at suitable employment or faithfully pursue a course of study or vocational training that will equip him for suitable employment.

(2)   Undergo available medical or psychiatric treatment and remain in a specified institution if required for that purpose.

28

(3)   Attend or reside in a facility providing rehabilitation, instruction, recreation, or residence for persons on parole.

(4)   Support his dependents and meet other family responsibilities.

(5)   Refrain from possessing a firearm, destructive device, or other dangerous weapon unless granted written permission by the Commission or the parole officer.

(6)   Report to a parole officer at reasonable times and in a reasonable manner, as directed by the Commission or the parole officer.

(7)   Permit the parole officer to visit him at reasonable times at his home or elsewhere.

(8)   Remain within the geographic limits fixed by the Commission unless granted written permission to leave by the Commission or the parole officer.

(8a)   Remain in one or more specified places for a specified period or periods each day and wear a device that permits the defendant's compliance with the condition to be monitored electronically.

(8b)   Remain alcohol free, and prove such abstinence through evaluation by a continuous alcohol monitoring system of a type approved by the Division of Adult Correction of the Department of Public Safety.

(9)   Answer all reasonable inquiries by the parole officer and obtain prior approval from the parole officer for any change in address or employment.

(10)   Promptly notify the parole officer of any change in address or employment.

(11)   Submit at reasonable times to warrantless searches by a parole officer of the parolee's person and of the parolee's vehicle and premises while the parolee is present, for purposes reasonably related to the parole supervision. The Commission may not require as a condition of parole that the parolee submit to any other searches that would otherwise be unlawful. If the parolee has been convicted of an offense which is a reportable conviction as defined in G.S. 14-208.6(4), or which involves the physical, mental, or sexual abuse of a minor, warrantless searches of the parolee's computer or other electronic mechanism which may contain electronic data shall be considered reasonably

29

related to the parole supervision. Whenever the search consists of testing for the presence of illegal drugs, the parolee may also be required to reimburse the Division of Adult Correction of the Department of Public Safety for the actual cost of drug testing and drug screening, if the results are positive.

(11a)   Make restitution or reparation to an aggrieved party as provided in G.S. 148-57.1.

(11b)   Comply with an order from a court of competent jurisdiction regarding the payment of an obligation of the parolee in connection with any judgment rendered by the court.

(11c)   In the case of a parolee who was attending a basic skills program during incarceration, continue attending a basic skills program in pursuit of a General Education Development Degree or adult high school diploma.

(12)   Satisfy other conditions reasonably related to his rehabilitation.

(b1)   Mandatory Satellite-Based Monitoring Required as Condition of Parole for Certain Offenders. - If a parolee is in a category described by G.S. 14-208.40(a)(1) or G.S. 14-208.40(a)(2), the Commission must require as a condition of parole that the parolee submit to satellite-based monitoring pursuant to Part 5 of Article 27A of Chapter 14 of the General Statutes.

(c)   Supervision Fee. - The Commission must require as a condition of parole that the parolee pay a supervision fee of forty dollars ($40.00) per month. The Commission may exempt a parolee from this condition of parole only if it finds that requiring him to pay the fee will constitute an undue economic burden. The fee must be paid to the clerk of superior court of the county in which the parolee was convicted. The clerk must transmit any money collected pursuant to this subsection to the State to be deposited in the general fund of the State. In no event shall a person released on parole be required to pay more than one supervision fee per month.

(d)   Any fees or costs paid by the parolee in order to comply with the imposition of subdivision (8b) of subsection (b) of this section shall be paid to the clerk of court for the county in which the parolee was convicted. Fees or costs collected under this subsection shall be transmitted to the entity providing the continuous alcohol monitoring system. (1977, c. 711, s. 1; 1979, c. 749, s. 11; 1983, c. 562; 1985, c. 474, s. 6; 1987, c. 579, s. 3; c. 830, s. 17; 1989 (Reg. Sess., 1990), c. 1034, s. 2; 1991, c. 54, s. 1; 1991 (Reg. Sess., 1992), c. 1000,

30

s. 2; 1993, c. 538, s. 39; 1994, Ex. Sess., c. 24, s. 14(b); 2002-126, s. 29A.2(c); 2006-247, s. 15(h); 2006-253, s. 27; 2007-165, ss. 4, 5; 2007-213, s. 8; 2010-31, s. 19.3(c); 2011-145, s. 19.1(h).)

§ 15A-1375. Commencement of parole; multiple sentences.

A period of parole commences on the day the prisoner is released from imprisonment. Periods of parole run concurrently with any federal or State prison, jail, probation, or parole term to which the defendant is subject during the period. (1977, c. 711, s. 1.)

§ 15A-1376. Arrest and hearing on parole violation.

(a)   Arrest for Violation of Parole. - A parolee is subject to arrest by a law-enforcement officer or a parole officer for violation of conditions of parole only upon the issuance of an order of temporary or conditional revocation of parole by the Post-Release Supervision and Parole Commission. However, a parole revocation hearing under subsection (e) may be held without first arresting the parolee.

(b)   When and Where Preliminary Hearing on Parole Violation Required. - Unless the hearing required by subsection (e) is first held or a continuance is requested by the parolee, a preliminary hearing on parole violation must be held reasonably near the place of the alleged violation or arrest and within seven working days of the arrest of a parolee to determine whether there is probable cause to believe that he violated a condition of parole. Otherwise, the parolee must be released seven working days after his arrest to continue on parole pending a hearing. If the parolee is not within the State, his preliminary hearing is as prescribed by G.S. 148-65.1A.

(c)   Officers to Conduct Hearing. - The preliminary hearing on parole violation must be conducted by a judicial official, or by a hearing officer designated by the Post-Release Supervision and Parole Commission. No person employed by the Division of Adult Correction of the Department of Public Safety may serve as a hearing officer at a hearing provided in this section unless he is a member of the Post-Release Supervision and Parole Commission or is employed solely as a hearing officer.

(d)   Procedure for Preliminary Hearing on Parole Violation. - The Division of Adult Correction of the Department of Public Safety must give the parolee notice of the preliminary hearing and its purpose, including a statement of the violations alleged. At the hearing, the parolee may appear and speak in his own behalf, may present relevant information, and may, on request, personally question witnesses and adverse informants, unless the hearing officer finds good cause for not allowing confrontation. If the person holding the hearing determines there is probable cause to believe the parolee violated his parole, he must summarize the reasons for his determination and the evidence he relied on. Formal rules of evidence do not apply at the hearing. If probable cause is found, the parolee may be held in the custody of the Division of Adult Correction of the Department of Public Safety to serve the appropriate term of imprisonment, subject to the outcome of a revocation hearing under subsection (e).

(e)   Revocation Hearing. - Before finally revoking parole, the Post-Release Supervision and Parole Commission must, unless the parolee waived the hearing or the time limit, provide a hearing within 45 days of the parolee's reconfinement to determine whether to revoke parole finally. The Post-Release Supervision and Parole Commission must adopt rules governing the hearing. (1977, c. 711, s. 1; 1977, 2nd Sess., c. 1147, ss. 23-26; 1987, c. 827, s. 1; 1993, c. 538, s. 40; 1994, Ex. Sess., c. 24, s. 14(b); 1996, 2nd Ex. Sess., c. 18, s. 20.15(a); 2000-189, s. 2; 2011-145, s. 19.1(h).)

§ 15A-1377. Repealed by Session Laws 1977, 2nd Sess., c. 1147, s. 27.

§§ 15A-1378 through 15A-1380. Reserved for future codification purposes.

Article 85A.

Parole of Certain Convicted Felons.

§§ 15A-1380.1 through 15A-1380.4: Repealed by Session Laws 1993, c. 538, s. 24.

Article 85B.

Review of Sentences of Life Imprisonment Without Parole.

§ 15A-1380.5: Repealed by Session Laws 1998-212, s. 19.4(q).

Article 86.

Reports of Dispositions of Criminal Cases.

§ 15A-1381. Disposition defined.

As used in this Article, the term "disposition" means any action which results in termination or indeterminate suspension of the prosecution of a criminal charge. A disposition may be any one of the following actions:

(1)   A finding of no probable cause pursuant to G.S. 15A-511(c)(2);

(2)   An order of dismissal pursuant to G.S. 15A-604;

(3)   A finding of no probable cause pursuant to G.S. 15A-612(a)(3);

(4)   A return of not a true bill pursuant to G.S. 15A-629;

(5)   Repealed by Session Laws 1989, c. 688, s. 4;

(6)   Dismissal pursuant to G.S. 15A-931 or 15A-932;

(7)   Dismissal pursuant to G.S. 15A-954, 15A-955 or 15A-959;

(8)   Finding of a defendant's incapacity to proceed pursuant to G.S. 15A-1002 or dismissal of charges pursuant to G.S. 15A-1008;

(9)   Entry of a plea of guilty or no contest pursuant to G.S. 15A-1011, without regard to the sentence imposed upon the plea, and even though prayer for judgment on the plea be continued;

(10)   Dismissal pursuant to G.S. 15A-1227;

(11)   Return of verdict pursuant to G.S. 15A-1237, without regard to the sentence imposed upon such verdict and even though prayer for judgment on such verdict be continued. (1981, c. 862, s. 1; 1989, c. 688, s. 4.)

§ 15A-1382. Reports of disposition; fingerprints.

(a)   When the defendant is fingerprinted pursuant to G.S. 15A-502 prior to the disposition of the case, a report of the disposition of the charges shall be made to the State Bureau of Investigation on a form supplied by the State Bureau of Investigation within 60 days following disposition.

(b)   When a defendant is found guilty of any felony, regardless of the class of felony, a report of the disposition of the charges shall be made to the State Bureau of Investigation on a form supplied by the State Bureau of Investigation within 60 days following disposition. If a convicted felon was not fingerprinted pursuant to G.S. 15A-502 prior to the disposition of the case, his fingerprints shall be taken and submitted to the State Bureau of Investigation along with the report of the disposition of the charges on forms supplied by the State Bureau of Investigation. (1981, c. 862, s. 1.)

§ 15A-1382.1. Reports of disposition; domestic violence; child abuse; sentencing.

(a)   When a defendant is found guilty of an offense involving assault, communicating a threat, or any of the acts as defined in G.S. 50B-1(a), the presiding judge shall determine whether the defendant and victim had a personal relationship. If the judge determines that there was a personal relationship between the defendant and the victim, then the judge shall indicate on the form reflecting the judgment that the case involved domestic violence. The clerk of court shall insure that the official record of the defendant's conviction includes the court's determination, so that any inquiry into the defendant's criminal record will reflect that the offense involved domestic violence.

(a1)   When a defendant is found guilty of an offense involving child abuse or is found guilty of an offense involving assault or any of the acts as defined in G.S. 50B-1(a) and the offense was committed against a minor, then the judge

34

shall indicate on the form reflecting the judgment that the case involved child abuse. The clerk of court shall ensure that the official record of the defendant's conviction includes the court's determination, so that any inquiry into the defendant's criminal record will reflect that the offense involved child abuse.

(b)   Repealed by Session Laws 2012-39, s. 2, effective December 1, 2012, and applicable to defendants placed on probation on or after that date.

(c)   The following definitions apply to this section:

(1)   "An offense involving assault" includes any offense where an assault occurred, whether or not the conviction is for an offense under Article 8 of Chapter 14 of the General Statutes.

(2)   "Inquiry" shall include any lawful review of the criminal records of persons convicted of an offense in this State, whether by law enforcement personnel or by private individuals.

(3)   "Personal relationship" is as defined in G.S. 50B-1(b). (2004-186, s. 11.1; 2012-39, s. 2; 2013-35, s. 2; 2013-123, s. 2.)

§ 15A-1382.2. Sentencing court to include in judgment whether firearm was used.

When a person is found guilty of a felony offense, the presiding judge shall determine whether the defendant used or displayed a firearm while committing the felony. If the judge determines that the defendant used or displayed a firearm while committing the felony, the sentencing court shall include that fact when entering the judgment that imposes the sentence for the felony conviction. (2013-369, s. 27.)

§ 15A-1383. Plans for implementation of Article; punishment for failure to comply; modification of plan.

(a)   On January 1, 1982, or on the first day of the month following the date on which any superior court district becomes effective under G.S. 7A-41, each senior resident superior court judge shall file a plan with the Director of the State

Bureau of Investigation for the implementation of the provisions of this Article. The plan shall be entered as an order of the court on that date. In drawing up the plan, the senior resident superior court judge may consult with any public official having authority within his district or set of districts as defined in G.S. 7A-41.1(a) and with any other persons as he may deem appropriate. Upon the request of the senior resident superior court judge, the State Bureau of Investigation shall provide such technical assistance in the preparation of the plan as the judge desires.

(b)   A person who is charged by the plan with a duty to make reports who fails to make such reports as required by the plan is punishable for civil contempt under Article 2 of Chapter 5A of the General Statutes.

(c)   When the senior resident superior court judge modifies, alters or amends a plan under this Article, the order making such modification, alteration or amendment shall be filed with the Director of the State Bureau of Investigation within 10 days of its entry.

(d)   Plans prepared under this Article are not "rules" within the meaning of Chapter 150B of the General Statutes. (1981, c. 862, s. 1; 1987 (Reg. Sess., 1988), c. 1037, s. 70; 1989, c. 770, s. 4; 2010-96, s. 6.)

§§ 15A-1384 through 15A-1390. Reserved for future codification purposes.

Article 87.

§§ 15A-1391 through 15A-1400. Reserved for future codification purposes.

SUBCHAPTER XIV. CORRECTION OF ERRORS AND APPEAL.

Article 88.

Post-Trial Motions and Appeal.

§ 15A-1401. Post-trial motions and appeal.

Relief from errors committed in criminal trials and proceedings and other post-trial relief may be sought by:

(1)   Motion for appropriate relief, as provided in Article 89.

(1a)   Motion for innocence claim inquiry as provided in Article 92 of Chapter 15A of the General Statutes.

(2)   Appeal and trial de novo in misdemeanor cases, as provided in Article 90.

(3)   Appeal, as provided in Article 91. (1977, c. 711, s. 1; 2006-184, s. 2; 2010-171, s. 5.)

§§ 15A-1402 through 15A-1410. Reserved for future codification purposes.

Article 89.

Motion for Appropriate Relief and Other Post-Trial Relief.

§ 15A-1411. Motion for appropriate relief.

(a)   Relief from errors committed in the trial division, or other post-trial relief, may be sought by a motion for appropriate relief. Procedure for the making of the motion is as set out in G.S. 15A-1420.

(b)   A motion for appropriate relief, whether made before or after the entry of judgment, is a motion in the original cause and not a new proceeding.

(c)   The relief formerly available by motion in arrest of judgment, motion to set aside the verdict, motion for new trial, post-conviction proceedings, coram nobis and all other post-trial motions is available by motion for appropriate relief. The availability of relief by motion for appropriate relief is not a bar to relief by writ of habeas corpus.

(d)   A claim of factual innocence asserted through the North Carolina Innocence Inquiry Commission does not constitute a motion for appropriate relief and does not impact rights or relief provided for in this Article. (1977, c. 711, s. 1; 2006-184, s. 4; 2010-171, s. 5.)

37

§ 15A-1412. Provisions of Article procedural.

The provision in this Article for the right to seek relief by motion for appropriate relief is procedural and is not determinative of the question of whether the moving party is entitled to the relief sought or to other appropriate relief. (1977, c. 711, s. 1.)

§ 15A-1413. Trial judges empowered to act; assignment of motions for appropriate relief.

(a)   A motion for appropriate relief made pursuant to G.S. 15A-1415 may be heard and determined in the trial division by any judge who (i) is empowered to act in criminal matters in the district court district as defined in G.S. 7A-133 or superior court district or set of districts as defined in G.S. 7A-41.1, as the case may be, in which the judgment was entered and (ii) is assigned pursuant to this section to review the motion for appropriate relief and take the appropriate administrative action to dispense with the motion.

(b)   The judge who presided at the trial is empowered to act upon a motion for appropriate relief made pursuant to G.S. 15A-1414. The judge may act even though the judge is in another district or even though the judge's commission has expired; however, if the judge who presided at the trial is still unavailable to act, the senior resident superior court judge or the chief district court judge, as appropriate, shall assign a judge who is empowered to act under subsection (a) of this section.

(c)   Repealed by Session Laws 2012-168, s. 2(a), effective December 1, 2012.

(d)   All motions for appropriate relief filed in superior court shall, when filed, be referred to the senior resident superior court judge, who shall assign the motion as provided by this section for review and administrative action, including, as may be appropriate, dismissal, calendaring for hearing, entry of a scheduling order for subsequent events in the case, or other appropriate actions.

All motions for appropriate relief filed in district court shall, when filed, be referred to the chief district court judge, who shall assign the motion as provided by this section for review and administrative action, including, as may be

38

appropriate, dismissal, calendaring for hearing, entry of a scheduling order for subsequent events in the case, or other appropriate actions.

(e)　　The assignment of a motion for appropriate relief filed under G.S. 15A-1415 is in the discretion of the senior resident superior court judge or chief district court judge as appropriate. (1977, c. 711, s. 1; 1987 (Reg. Sess., 1988), c. 1037, s. 71; 2012-168, s. 2(a).)

§ 15A-1414. Motion by defendant for appropriate relief made within 10 days after verdict.

(a)　　After the verdict but not more than 10 days after entry of judgment, the defendant by motion may seek appropriate relief for any error committed during or prior to the trial.

(b)　　Unless included in G.S. 15A-1415, all errors, including but not limited to the following, must be asserted within 10 days after entry of judgment:

(1)　　Any error of law, including the following:

a.　　The court erroneously failed to dismiss the charge prior to trial pursuant to G.S. 15A-954.

b.　　The court's ruling was contrary to law with regard to motions made before or during the trial, or with regard to the admission or exclusion of evidence.

c.　　The evidence, at the close of all the evidence, was insufficient to justify submission of the case to the jury, whether or not a motion so asserting was made before verdict.

d.　　The court erroneously instructed the jury.

(2)　　The verdict is contrary to the weight of the evidence.

(3)　　For any other cause the defendant did not receive a fair and impartial trial.

(4)   The sentence imposed on the defendant is not supported by evidence introduced at the trial and sentencing hearing. This motion must be addressed to the sentencing judge.

(c)   The motion may be made and acted upon in the trial court whether or not notice of appeal has been given. (1977, c. 711, s. 1; 1979, c. 760, s. 3; 1981, c. 179, s. 6.)

§ 15A-1415. Grounds for appropriate relief which may be asserted by defendant after verdict; limitation as to time.

(a)   At any time after verdict, a noncapital defendant by motion may seek appropriate relief upon any of the grounds enumerated in this section. In a capital case, a postconviction motion for appropriate relief shall be filed within 120 days from the latest of the following:

(1)   The court's judgment has been filed, but the defendant failed to perfect a timely appeal;

(2)   The mandate issued by a court of the appellate division on direct appeal pursuant to N.C.R. App. P. 32(b) and the time for filing a petition for writ of certiorari to the United States Supreme Court has expired without a petition being filed;

(3)   The United States Supreme Court denied a timely petition for writ of certiorari of the decision on direct appeal by the Supreme Court of North Carolina;

(4)   Following the denial of discretionary review by the Supreme Court of North Carolina, the United States Supreme Court denied a timely petition for writ of certiorari seeking review of the decision on direct appeal by the North Carolina Court of Appeals;

(5)   The United States Supreme Court granted the defendant's or the State's timely petition for writ of certiorari of the decision on direct appeal by the Supreme Court of North Carolina or North Carolina Court of Appeals, but subsequently left the defendant's conviction and sentence undisturbed; or

(6)   The appointment of postconviction counsel for an indigent capital defendant.

(b)   The following are the only grounds which the defendant may assert by a motion for appropriate relief made more than 10 days after entry of judgment:

(1)   The acts charged in the criminal pleading did not at the time they were committed constitute a violation of criminal law.

(2)   The trial court lacked jurisdiction over the person of the defendant or over the subject matter.

(3)   The conviction was obtained in violation of the Constitution of the United States or the Constitution of North Carolina.

(4)   The defendant was convicted or sentenced under a statute that was in violation of the Constitution of the United States or the Constitution of North Carolina.

(5)   The conduct for which the defendant was prosecuted was protected by the Constitution of the United States or the Constitution of North Carolina.

(6)   Repealed by Session Laws 1995 (Regular Session, 1996), c. 719, s. 1, effective June 21, 1996.

(7)   There has been a significant change in law, either substantive or procedural, applied in the proceedings leading to the defendant's conviction or sentence, and retroactive application of the changed legal standard is required.

(8)   The sentence imposed was unauthorized at the time imposed, contained a type of sentence disposition or a term of imprisonment not authorized for the particular class of offense and prior record or conviction level was illegally imposed, or is otherwise invalid as a matter of law. However, a motion for appropriate relief on the grounds that the sentence imposed on the defendant is not supported by evidence introduced at the trial and sentencing hearing must be made before the sentencing judge.

(9)   The defendant is in confinement and is entitled to release because his sentence has been fully served.

(10)   The defendant was convicted of a first offense of prostitution under G.S. 14-204, and the court did not discharge the defendant and dismiss the charge pursuant to G.S. 14-204(b); the defendant's participation in the offense was a result of having been a victim of human trafficking under G.S. 14-43.11, sexual servitude under G.S. 14-43.13, or the federal Trafficking Victims Protection Act (22 U.S.C. § 7102(13)); and the defendant seeks to have the conviction vacated.

(c)   Notwithstanding the time limitations herein, a defendant at any time after verdict may by a motion for appropriate relief, raise the ground that evidence is available which was unknown or unavailable to the defendant at the time of trial, which could not with due diligence have been discovered or made available at that time, including recanted testimony, and which has a direct and material bearing upon the defendant's eligibility for the death penalty or the defendant's guilt or innocence. A motion based upon such newly discovered evidence must be filed within a reasonable time of its discovery.

(d)   For good cause shown, the defendant may be granted an extension of time to file the motion for appropriate relief. The presumptive length of an extension of time under this subsection is up to 30 days, but can be longer if the court finds extraordinary circumstances.

(e)   Where a defendant alleges ineffective assistance of prior trial or appellate counsel as a ground for the illegality of his conviction or sentence, he shall be deemed to waive the attorney-client privilege with respect to both oral and written communications between such counsel and the defendant to the extent the defendant's prior counsel reasonably believes such communications are necessary to defend against the allegations of ineffectiveness. This waiver of the attorney-client privilege shall be automatic upon the filing of the motion for appropriate relief alleging ineffective assistance of prior counsel, and the superior court need not enter an order waiving the privilege.

(f)   In the case of a defendant who is represented by counsel in postconviction proceedings in superior court, the defendant's prior trial or appellate counsel shall make available to the defendant's counsel their complete files relating to the case of the defendant. The State, to the extent allowed by law, shall make available to the defendant's counsel the complete files of all law enforcement and prosecutorial agencies involved in the investigation of the crimes committed or the prosecution of the defendant. If the State has a reasonable belief that allowing inspection of any portion of the files by counsel for the defendant would not be in the interest of justice, the State may submit for

42

inspection by the court those portions of the files so identified. If upon examination of the files, the court finds that the files could not assist the defendant in investigating, preparing, or presenting a motion for appropriate relief, the court in its discretion may allow the State to withhold that portion of the files.

(g)   The defendant may file amendments to a motion for appropriate relief at least 30 days prior to the commencement of a hearing on the merits of the claims asserted in the motion or at any time before the date for the hearing has been set, whichever is later. Where the defendant has filed an amendment to a motion for appropriate relief, the State shall, upon request, be granted a continuance of 30 days before the date of hearing. After such hearing has begun, the defendant may file amendments only to conform the motion to evidence adduced at the hearing, or to raise claims based on such evidence. (1977, c. 711, s. 1; 1981, c. 179, s. 7; 1993, c. 538, s. 25; 1994, Ex. Sess., c. 24, s. 14(b); 1995 (Reg. Sess., 1996), c. 719, s. 1; 2009-517, s. 2; 2013-368, s. 9.)

§ 15A-1416. Motion by the State for appropriate relief.

(a)   After the verdict but not more than 10 days after entry of judgment, the State by motion may seek appropriate relief for any error which it may assert upon appeal.

(b)   At any time after verdict the State may make a motion for appropriate relief for:

(1)   The imposition of sentence when prayer for judgment has been continued and grounds for the imposition of sentence are asserted.

(2)   The initiation of any proceeding authorized under Article 82, Probation; Article 83, Imprisonment; and Article 84, Fines, with regard to the modification of sentences. The procedural provisions of those Articles are controlling. (1977, c. 711, s. 1.)

§ 15A-1416.1. Motion by the defendant to vacate prostitution conviction for sex trafficking victim.

(a)   A motion for appropriate relief seeking to vacate a conviction for prostitution based on the grounds set out in G.S. 15A-1415(b)(10) shall be filed in the court where the conviction occurred. The motion may be filed at any time following the entry of a verdict or finding of guilty under G.S. 14-204. Any motion for appropriate relief filed under this section shall state why the facts giving rise to this motion were not presented to the trial court and shall be made with due diligence after the defendant has ceased to be a victim of such trafficking or has sought services for victims of such offenses, subject to reasonable concerns for the safety of the defendant, family members of the defendant, or other victims of such trafficking that may be jeopardized by the bringing of such motion or for other reasons consistent with the purpose of this section. Reasonable notice of the motion shall be served upon the State.

(b)   The court may grant the motion if, in the discretion of the court, the violation was a result of the defendant having been a victim of human trafficking or sexual servitude. Evidence of such may include any of the following documents listed in subdivisions (1) through (3) of this subsection; alternatively, the court may consider such other evidence as it deems of sufficient credibility and probative value in determining whether the defendant is a trafficking victim:

(1)   Certified records of federal or State court proceedings which demonstrate that the defendant was a victim of a person charged with an offense under G.S. 14-43.11, G.S. 14-43.13, or under 22 U.S.C. Chapter 78.

(2)   Certified records of "approval notices" or "enforcement certifications" generated from federal immigration proceedings available to such victims.

(3)   A sworn statement from a trained professional staff of a victim services organization, an attorney, a member of the clergy, or a medical or other professional from whom the defendant has sought assistance in addressing the trauma associated with being trafficked.

(c)   If the court grants a motion under this section, the court must vacate the conviction and may take such additional action as is appropriate in the circumstances. (2013-368, s. 10.)

§ 15A-1417. Relief available.

44

(a)   The following relief is available when the court grants a motion for appropriate relief:

(1)   New trial on all or any of the charges.

(2)   Dismissal of all or any of the charges.

(3)   The relief sought by the State pursuant to G.S. 15A-1416.

(3a)   For claims of factual innocence, referral to the North Carolina Innocence Inquiry Commission established by Article 92 of Chapter 15A of the General Statutes.

(4)   Any other appropriate relief.

(b)   When relief is granted in the trial court and the offense is divided into degrees or necessarily includes lesser offenses, and the court is of the opinion that the evidence does not sustain the verdict but is sufficient to sustain a finding of guilty of a lesser degree or of a lesser offense necessarily included in the one charged, the court may, with consent of the State, accept a plea of guilty to the lesser degree or lesser offense.

(c)   If resentencing is required, the trial division may enter an appropriate sentence. If a motion is granted in the appellate division and resentencing is required, the case must be remanded to the trial division for entry of a new sentence. (1977, c. 711, s. 1; 2006-184, s. 3; 2010-171, s. 5.)

§ 15A-1418. Motion for appropriate relief in the appellate division.

(a)   When a case is in the appellate division for review, a motion for appropriate relief based upon grounds set out in G.S. 15A-1415 must be made in the appellate division. For the purpose of this section a case is in the appellate division when the jurisdiction of the trial court has been divested as provided in G.S. 15A-1448, or when a petition for a writ of certiorari has been granted. When a petition for a writ of certiorari has been filed but not granted, a copy or written statement of any motion made in the trial court, and of any disposition of the motion, must be filed in the appellate division.

(b)   When a motion for appropriate relief is made in the appellate division, the appellate court must decide whether the motion may be determined on the basis of the materials before it, whether it is necessary to remand the case to the trial division for taking evidence or conducting other proceedings, or, for claims of factual innocence, whether to refer the case for further investigation to the North Carolina Innocence Inquiry Commission established by Article 92 of Chapter 15A of the General Statutes. If the appellate court does not remand the case for proceedings on the motion, it may determine the motion in conjunction with the appeal and enter its ruling on the motion with its determination of the case.

(c)   The order of remand must provide that the time periods for perfecting or proceeding with the appeal are tolled, and direct that the order of the trial division with regard to the motion be transmitted to the appellate division so that it may proceed with the appeal or enter an appropriate order terminating it. (1977, c. 711, s. 1; 2006-184, s. 5; 2010-171, s. 5.)

§ 15A-1419. When motion for appropriate relief denied.

(a)   The following are grounds for the denial of a motion for appropriate relief, including motions filed in capital cases:

(1)   Upon a previous motion made pursuant to this Article, the defendant was in a position to adequately raise the ground or issue underlying the present motion but did not do so. This subdivision does not apply when the previous motion was made within 10 days after entry of judgment or the previous motion was made during the pendency of the direct appeal.

(2)   The ground or issue underlying the motion was previously determined on the merits upon an appeal from the judgment or upon a previous motion or proceeding in the courts of this State or a federal court, unless since the time of such previous determination there has been a retroactively effective change in the law controlling such issue.

(3)   Upon a previous appeal the defendant was in a position to adequately raise the ground or issue underlying the present motion but did not do so.

(4)   The defendant failed to file a timely motion for appropriate relief as required by G.S. 15A-1415(a).

(b)   The court shall deny the motion under any of the circumstances specified in this section, unless the defendant can demonstrate:

(1)   Good cause for excusing the grounds for denial listed in subsection (a) of this section and can demonstrate actual prejudice resulting from the defendant's claim; or

(2)   That failure to consider the defendant's claim will result in a fundamental miscarriage of justice.

(c)   For the purposes of subsection (b) of this section, good cause may only be shown if the defendant establishes by a preponderance of the evidence that his failure to raise the claim or file a timely motion was:

(1)   The result of State action in violation of the United States Constitution or the North Carolina Constitution including ineffective assistance of trial or appellate counsel;

(2)   The result of the recognition of a new federal or State right which is retroactively applicable; or

(3)   Based on a factual predicate that could not have been discovered through the exercise of reasonable diligence in time to present the claim on a previous State or federal postconviction review.

A trial attorney's ignorance of a claim, inadvertence, or tactical decision to withhold a claim may not constitute good cause, nor may a claim of ineffective assistance of prior postconviction counsel constitute good cause.

(d)   For the purposes of subsection (b) of this section, actual prejudice may only be shown if the defendant establishes by a preponderance of the evidence that an error during the trial or sentencing worked to the defendant's actual and substantial disadvantage, raising a reasonable probability, viewing the record as a whole, that a different result would have occurred but for the error.

(e)   For the purposes of subsection (b) of this section, a fundamental miscarriage of justice only results if:

(1)   The defendant establishes that more likely than not, but for the error, no reasonable fact finder would have found the defendant guilty of the underlying offense; or

(2)   The defendant establishes by clear and convincing evidence that, but for the error, no reasonable fact finder would have found the defendant eligible for the death penalty.

A defendant raising a claim of newly discovered evidence of factual innocence or ineligibility for the death penalty, otherwise barred by the provisions of subsection (a) of this section or G.S. 15A-1415(c), may only show a fundamental miscarriage of justice by proving by clear and convincing evidence that, in light of the new evidence, if credible, no reasonable juror would have found the defendant guilty beyond a reasonable doubt or eligible for the death penalty. (1977, c. 711, s. 1; 1995 (Reg. Sess., 1996), c. 719, s. 2.)

§ 15A-1420. Motion for appropriate relief; procedure.

(a)   Form, Service, Filing. -

(1)   A motion for appropriate relief must:

a.   Be made in writing unless it is made:

1.   In open court;

2.   Before the judge who presided at trial;

3.   Before the end of the session if made in superior court; and

4.   Within 10 days after entry of judgment;

b.   State the grounds for the motion;

c.   Set forth the relief sought;

c1.   If the motion for appropriate relief is being made in superior court and is being made by an attorney, the attorney must certify in writing that there is a sound legal basis for the motion and that it is being made in good faith; and that the attorney has notified both the district attorney's office and the attorney who initially represented the defendant of the motion; and further, that the attorney has reviewed the trial transcript or made a good-faith determination that the nature of the relief sought in the motion does not require that the trial transcript be read in its entirety. In the event that the trial transcript is unavailable, instead of certifying that the attorney has read the trial transcript, the attorney shall set forth in writing what efforts were undertaken to locate the transcript; and

d.   Be timely filed.

(2)   A written motion for appropriate relief must be served in the manner provided in G.S. 15A-951(b). When a motion for appropriate relief is permitted to be made orally the court must determine whether the matter may be heard immediately or at a later time. If the opposing party, or his counsel if he is represented, is not present, the court must provide for the giving of adequate notice of the motion and the date of hearing to the opposing party, or his counsel if he is represented by counsel.

(3)   A written motion for appropriate relief must be filed in the manner provided in G.S. 15A-951(c).

(4)   An oral or written motion for appropriate relief may not be granted in district court without the signature of the district attorney, indicating that the State has had an opportunity to consent or object to the motion. However, the court may grant a motion for appropriate relief without the district attorney's signature 10 business days after the district attorney has been notified in open court of the motion, or served with the motion pursuant to G.S. 15A-951(c).

(5)   An oral or written motion for appropriate relief made in superior court and made by an attorney may not be granted by the court unless the attorney has complied with the requirements of sub-subdivision c1. of subdivision (1) of this subsection.

(b)   Supporting Affidavits. -

(1)   A motion for appropriate relief made after the entry of judgment must be supported by affidavit or other documentary evidence if based upon the existence or occurrence of facts which are not ascertainable from the records and any transcript of the case or which are not within the knowledge of the judge who hears the motion.

(2)   The opposing party may file affidavits or other documentary evidence.

(b1)   Filing Motion With Clerk. -

(1)	The proceeding shall be commenced by filing with the clerk of superior court of the district wherein the defendant was indicted a motion, with service on the district attorney in noncapital cases, and service on both the district attorney and Attorney General in capital cases.

(2)	The clerk, upon receipt of the motion, shall place the motion on the criminal docket. When a motion is placed on the criminal docket, the clerk shall promptly bring the motion, or a copy of the motion, to the attention of the senior resident superior court judge or chief district court judge, as appropriate, for assignment to the appropriate judge pursuant to G.S. 15A-1413.

(b2)	Repealed by Session Laws 2013-385, s. 3.1, effective December 1, 2013.

(b3)	Repealed by Session Laws 2013-385, s. 3.1, effective December 1, 2013.

(c)	Hearings, Showing of Prejudice; Findings. -

(1)	Any party is entitled to a hearing on questions of law or fact arising from the motion and any supporting or opposing information presented unless the court determines that the motion is without merit. The court must determine, on the basis of these materials and the requirements of this subsection, whether an evidentiary hearing is required to resolve questions of fact. Upon the motion of either party, the judge may direct the attorneys for the parties to appear before him for a conference on any prehearing matter in the case.

(2)	An evidentiary hearing is not required when the motion is made in the trial court pursuant to G.S. 15A-1414, but the court may hold an evidentiary hearing if it is appropriate to resolve questions of fact.

(3)	The court must determine the motion without an evidentiary hearing when the motion and supporting and opposing information present only questions of law. The defendant has no right to be present at such a hearing where only questions of law are to be argued.

(4)	If the court cannot rule upon the motion without the hearing of evidence, it must conduct a hearing for the taking of evidence, and must make findings of fact. The defendant has a right to be present at the evidentiary hearing and to be represented by counsel. A waiver of the right to be present must be in writing.

(5)   If an evidentiary hearing is held, the moving party has the burden of proving by a preponderance of the evidence every fact essential to support the motion.

(6)   A defendant who seeks relief by motion for appropriate relief must show the existence of the asserted ground for relief. Relief must be denied unless prejudice appears, in accordance with G.S. 15A-1443.

(7)   The court must rule upon the motion and enter its order accordingly. When the motion is based upon an asserted violation of the rights of the defendant under the Constitution or laws or treaties of the United States, the court must make and enter conclusions of law and a statement of the reasons for its determination to the extent required, when taken with other records and transcripts in the case, to indicate whether the defendant has had a full and fair hearing on the merits of the grounds so asserted.

(d)   Action on Court's Own Motion. - At any time that a defendant would be entitled to relief by motion for appropriate relief, the court may grant such relief upon its own motion. The court must cause appropriate notice to be given to the parties.

(e)   Nothing in this section shall prevent the parties to the action from entering into an agreement for appropriate relief, including an agreement as to any aspect, procedural or otherwise, of a motion for appropriate relief. (1965, c. 352, s. 1; 1973, c. 47, s. 2; 1977, c. 711, s. 1; 1995 (Reg. Sess., 1996), c. 719, ss. 3, 4; 2006-253, s. 30; 2009-517, s. 1; 2012-168, s. 2(b); 2013-385, s. 3.1.)

§ 15A-1421. Indigent defendants.

The provisions of Chapter 7A of the General Statutes with regard to the appointment of counsel for indigent defendants are applicable to proceedings under this Article. The court also may make appropriate orders relieving indigent defendants of all or a portion of the costs of the proceedings. (1977, c. 711, s. 1.)

§ 15A-1422. Review upon appeal.

(a)   The making of a motion for appropriate relief is not a prerequisite for asserting an error upon appeal.

(b)   The grant or denial of relief sought pursuant to G.S. 15A-1414 is subject to appellate review only in an appeal regularly taken.

(c)   The court's ruling on a motion for appropriate relief pursuant to G.S. 15A-1415 is subject to review:

(1)   If the time for appeal from the conviction has not expired, by appeal.

(2)   If an appeal is pending when the ruling is entered, in that appeal.

(3)   If the time for appeal has expired and no appeal is pending, by writ of certiorari.

(d)   There is no right to appeal from the denial of a motion for appropriate relief when the movant is entitled to a trial de novo upon appeal.

(e)   When an error asserted upon appeal has also been the subject of a motion for appropriate relief, denial of the motion has no effect on the right to assert error upon appeal.

(f)   Decisions of the Court of Appeals on motions for appropriate relief that embrace matter set forth in G.S. 15A-1415(b) are final and not subject to further review by appeal, certification, writ, motion, or otherwise. (1977, c. 711, s. 1; 1981, c. 470, s. 3.)

§§ 15A-1423 through 15A-1430. Reserved for future codification purposes.

Article 90.

Appeals from Magistrates and District Court Judges.

§ 15A-1431. Appeals by defendants from magistrate and district court judge; trial de novo.

(a)   A defendant convicted before a magistrate may appeal for trial de novo before a district court judge without a jury.

52

(b)   A defendant convicted in the district court before the judge may appeal to the superior court for trial de novo with a jury as provided by law. Upon the docketing in the superior court of an appeal from a judgment imposed pursuant to a plea arrangement between the State and the defendant, the jurisdiction of the superior court over any misdemeanor dismissed, reduced, or modified pursuant to that plea arrangement shall be the same as was had by the district court prior to the plea arrangement.

(c)   Within 10 days of entry of judgment, notice of appeal may be given orally in open court or in writing to the clerk. Within 10 days of entry of judgment, the defendant may withdraw his appeal and comply with the judgment. Upon expiration of the 10-day period, if an appeal has been entered and not withdrawn, the clerk must transfer the case to the appropriate court.

(d)   A defendant convicted by a magistrate or district court judge is not barred from appeal because of compliance with the judgment, but notice of appeal after compliance must be given by the defendant in person to the magistrate or judge who heard the case or, if he is not available, notice must be given:

(1)   Before a magistrate in the county, in the case of appeals from the magistrate; or

(2)   During an open session of district court in the district court district as defined in G.S. 7A-133, in the case of appeals from district court.

The magistrate or district court judge must review the case and fix conditions of pretrial release as appropriate. If a defendant has paid a fine or costs and then appeals, the amount paid must be remitted to the defendant, but the judge, clerk or magistrate to whom notice of appeal is given may order the remission delayed pending the determination of the appeal.

(e)   Any order of pretrial release remains in effect pending appeal by the defendant unless the judge modifies the order.

(f)   Repealed by Session Laws 2005-339, s. 1, effective August 26, 2005.

(f1)   Appeal pursuant to this section stays the execution of all portions of the judgment, including all of the following:

(1)   Payment of costs.

(2)   Payment of a fine.

(3)   Probation or special probation.

(4)   Active punishment.

Pursuant to subsection (e) of this section, however, the judge may order any appropriate condition of pretrial release, including confinement in a local confinement facility, pending the trial de novo in superior court.

(g)   The defendant may withdraw his appeal at any time prior to calendaring of the case for trial de novo. The case is then automatically remanded to the court from which the appeal was taken, for execution of the judgment.

(h)   The defendant may withdraw his appeal after the calendaring of the case for trial de novo only by consent of the court, and with the attachment of costs of that court, unless the costs or any part of the costs are remitted by the court. The case may then be remanded by order of the court to the court from which the appeal was taken for execution of the judgment with any additional court costs that attached and that have not been remitted. (1977, c. 711, s. 1; 1979, c. 758, p. 2; 1979, 2nd Sess., c. 1328, s. 1; 1987 (Reg. Sess., 1988), c. 1037, s. 72; 1991, c. 63, s. 1; 2005-339, s. 1.)

§ 15A-1432. Appeals by State from district court judge.

(a)   Unless the rule against double jeopardy prohibits further prosecution, the State may appeal from the district court judge to the superior court:

(1)   When there has been a decision or judgment dismissing criminal charges as to one or more counts.

(2)   Upon the granting of a motion for a new trial on the ground of newly discovered or newly available evidence but only on questions of law.

(b)   When the State appeals pursuant to subsection (a) the appeal is by written motion specifying the basis of the appeal made within 10 days after the entry of the judgment in the district court. The motion must be filed with the clerk and a copy served upon the defendant.

54

(c)   The motion may be heard by any judge of superior court having authority for the trial of criminal cases in the district. The State and the defendant are entitled to file briefs and are entitled to adequate time for their preparation, consonant with the expeditious handling of the appeal.

(d)   If the superior court finds that a judgment, ruling, or order dismissing criminal charges in the district court was in error, it must reinstate the charges and remand the matter to district court for further proceedings. The defendant may appeal this order to the appellate division as in the case of other orders of the superior court, including by an interlocutory appeal if the defendant, or his attorney, certifies to the superior court judge who entered the order that the appeal is not taken for the purpose of delay and if the judge finds the cause is appropriately justiciable in the appellate division as an interlocutory matter.

(e)   If the superior court finds that the order of the district court was correct, it must enter an order affirming the judgment of the district court. The State may appeal the order of the superior court to the appellate division upon certificate by the district attorney to the judge who affirmed the judgment that the appeal is not taken for the purpose of delay. (1977, c. 711, s. 1; 1987, c. 398.)

§§ 15A-1433 through 15A-1440. Reserved for future codification purposes.

Article 91.

Appeal to Appellate Division.

§ 15A-1441. Correction of errors by appellate division.

Errors of law may be corrected upon appellate review as provided in this Article, except that review of capital cases shall be given priority on direct appeal and in State postconviction proceedings. (1977, c. 711, s. 1; 1995 (Reg. Sess., 1996), c. 719, s. 6.)

§ 15A-1442. Grounds for correction of error by appellate division.

The following constitute grounds for correction of errors by the appellate division.

(1)   Lack of Jurisdiction. -

a.   The trial court lacked jurisdiction over the offense.

b.   The trial court did not have jurisdiction over the person of the defendant.

(2)   Error in the Criminal Pleading. - Failure to charge a crime, in that:

a.   The criminal pleading charged acts which at the time they were committed did not constitute a violation of criminal law; or

b.   The pleading fails to state essential elements of an alleged violation as required by G.S. 15A-924(a)(5).

(3)   Insufficiency of the Evidence. - The evidence was insufficient as a matter of law.

(4)   Errors in Procedure. -

a.   There has been a denial of pretrial motions or relief to which the defendant is entitled, so as to affect the defendant's preparation or presentation of his defense, to his prejudice.

b.   There has been a denial of a trial motion or relief to which the defendant is entitled, to his prejudice.

c.   There has been error in the admission or exclusion of evidence, to the prejudice of the defendant.

d.   There has been error in the judge's instructions to the jury, to the prejudice of the defendant.

e.   There has been a denial of a post-trial motion or relief to which the defendant is entitled, to his prejudice. This provision is subject to the provisions of G.S. 15A-1422.

(5)   Constitutionally Invalid Procedure or Statute; Prosecution for Constitutionally Protected Conduct. -

56

a.   The conviction was obtained by a violation of the Constitution of the United States or of the Constitution of North Carolina.

b.   The defendant was convicted under a statute that is in violation of the Constitution of the United States or the Constitution of North Carolina.

c.   The conduct for which the defendant was prosecuted was protected by the Constitution of the United States or the Constitution of North Carolina.

(5a)   Insufficient Basis for Sentence. - The sentence imposed on the defendant is not supported by evidence introduced at the trial and sentencing hearing.

(5b)   Violation of Sentencing Structure. - The sentence imposed:

a.   Results from an incorrect finding of the defendant's prior record level under G.S. 15A-1340.14 or the defendant's prior conviction level under G.S. 15A-1340.21;

b.   Contains a type of sentence disposition that is not authorized by G.S. 15A-1340.17 or G.S. 15A-1340.23 for the defendant's class of offense and prior record or conviction level; or

c.   Contains a term of imprisonment that is for a duration not authorized by G.S. 15A-1340.17 or G.S. 15A-1340.23 for the defendant's class or offense and prior record or conviction level.

(6)   Other Errors of Law. - Any other error of law was committed by the trial court to the prejudice of the defendant. (1977, c. 711, s. 1; 1979, c. 760, s. 3; 1993, c. 538, s. 26; 1994, Ex. Sess., c. 24, s. 14(b).)

§ 15A-1443. Existence and showing of prejudice.

(a)   A defendant is prejudiced by errors relating to rights arising other than under the Constitution of the United States when there is a reasonable possibility that, had the error in question not been committed, a different result would have been reached at the trial out of which the appeal arises. The burden of showing such prejudice under this subsection is upon the defendant.

Prejudice also exists in any instance in which it is deemed to exist as a matter of law or error is deemed reversible per se.

(b)   A violation of the defendant's rights under the Constitution of the United States is prejudicial unless the appellate court finds that it was harmless beyond a reasonable doubt. The burden is upon the State to demonstrate, beyond a reasonable doubt, that the error was harmless.

(c)   A defendant is not prejudiced by the granting of relief which he has sought or by error resulting from his own conduct. (1977, c. 711, s. 1.)

§ 15A-1444. When defendant may appeal; certiorari.

(a)   A defendant who has entered a plea of not guilty to a criminal charge, and who has been found guilty of a crime, is entitled to appeal as a matter of right when final judgment has been entered.

(a1)   A defendant who has been found guilty, or entered a plea of guilty or no contest to a felony, is entitled to appeal as a matter of right the issue of whether his or her sentence is supported by evidence introduced at the trial and sentencing hearing only if the minimum sentence of imprisonment does not fall within the presumptive range for the defendant's prior record or conviction level and class of offense. Otherwise, the defendant is not entitled to appeal this issue as a matter of right but may petition the appellate division for review of this issue by writ of certiorari.

(a2)   A defendant who has entered a plea of guilty or no contest to a felony or misdemeanor in superior court is entitled to appeal as a matter of right the issue of whether the sentence imposed:

(1)   Results from an incorrect finding of the defendant's prior record level under G.S. 15A-1340.14 or the defendant's prior conviction level under G.S. 15A-1340.21;

(2)   Contains a type of sentence disposition that is not authorized by G.S. 15A-1340.17 or G.S. 15A-1340.23 for the defendant's class of offense and prior record or conviction level; or

58

(3)   Contains a term of imprisonment that is for a duration not authorized by G.S. 15A-1340.17 or G.S. 15A-1340.23 for the defendant's class of offense and prior record or conviction level.

(b)   Procedures for appeal from the magistrate to the district court are as provided in Article 90, Appeals from Magistrates and from District Court Judges.

(c)   Procedures for appeal from the district court to the superior court are as provided in Article 90, Appeals from Magistrates and from District Court Judges.

(d)   Procedures for appeal to the appellate division are as provided in this Article, the rules of the appellate division, and Chapter 7A of the General Statutes. The appeal must be perfected and conducted in accordance with the requirements of those provisions.

(e)   Except as provided in subsections (a1) and (a2) of this section and G.S. 15A-979, and except when a motion to withdraw a plea of guilty or no contest has been denied, the defendant is not entitled to appellate review as a matter of right when he has entered a plea of guilty or no contest to a criminal charge in the superior court, but he may petition the appellate division for review by writ of certiorari. If an indigent defendant petitions the appellate division for a writ of certiorari, the presiding superior court judge may in his discretion order the preparation of the record and transcript of the proceedings at the expense of the State.

(f)   The ruling of the court upon a motion for appropriate relief is subject to review upon appeal or by writ of certiorari as provided in G.S. 15A-1422.

(g)   Review by writ of certiorari is available when provided for by this Chapter, by other rules of law, or by rule of the appellate division. (1977, c. 711, s. 1; 1979, c. 760, s. 3; 1981, c. 179, ss. 8, 9; 1993, c. 538, s. 27; 1994, Ex. Sess., c. 24, s. 14(b); 1997-80, s. 4.)

§ 15A-1445. Appeal by the State.

(a)   Unless the rule against double jeopardy prohibits further prosecution, the State may appeal from the superior court to the appellate division:

(1)   When there has been a decision or judgment dismissing criminal charges as to one or more counts.

(2)   Upon the granting of a motion for a new trial on the ground of newly discovered or newly available evidence but only on questions of law.

(3)   When the State alleges that the sentence imposed:

a.   Results from an incorrect determination of the defendant's prior record level under G.S. 15A-1340.14 or the defendant's prior conviction level under G.S. 15A-1340.21;

b.   Contains a type of sentence disposition that is not authorized by G.S. 15A-1340.17 or G.S. 15A-1340.23 for the defendant's class of offense and prior record or conviction level;

c.   Contains a term of imprisonment that is for a duration not authorized by G.S. 15A-1340.17 or G.S. 15A-1340.23 for the defendant's class of offense and prior record or conviction level; or

d.   Imposes an intermediate punishment pursuant to G.S. 15A-1340.13(g) based on findings of extraordinary mitigating circumstances that are not supported by evidence or are insufficient as a matter of law to support the dispositional deviation.

(b)   The State may appeal an order by the superior court granting a motion to suppress as provided in G.S. 15A-979. (1977, c. 711, s. 1; 1993, c. 538, s. 28; 1994, Ex. Sess., c. 14, s. 28, c. 24, s. 14(b).)

§ 15A-1446. Requisites for preserving the right to appellate review.

(a)   Except as provided in subsection (d), error may not be asserted upon appellate review unless the error has been brought to the attention of the trial court by appropriate and timely objection or motion. No particular form is required in order to preserve the right to assert the alleged error upon appeal if the motion or objection clearly presented the alleged error to the trial court. Formal exceptions are not required, but when evidence is excluded a record must be made in the manner provided in G.S. 1A-1, Rule 43(c), in order to assert upon appeal error in the exclusion of that evidence.

(b)   Failure to make an appropriate and timely motion or objection constitutes a waiver of the right to assert the alleged error upon appeal, but the appellate court may review such errors affecting substantial rights in the interest of justice if it determines it appropriate to do so.

(c)   The making of post-trial motions is not a prerequisite to the assertion of error on appeal.

(d)   Errors based upon any of the following grounds, which are asserted to have occurred, may be the subject of appellate review even though no objection, exception or motion has been made in the trial division.

(1)   Lack of jurisdiction of the trial court over the offense of which the defendant was convicted.

(2)   Lack of jurisdiction of the trial court over the person of the defendant.

(3)   The criminal pleading charged acts which, at the time they were committed, did not constitute a violation of criminal law.

(4)   The pleading fails to state essential elements of an alleged violation, as required by G.S. 15A-924(a)(5).

(5)   The evidence was insufficient as a matter of law.

(6)   The defendant was convicted under a statute that is in violation of the Constitution of the United States or the Constitution of North Carolina.

(7)   Repealed by Session Laws 1977, 2nd Sess., c. 1147, s. 28.

(8)   The conduct for which the defendant was prosecuted was protected by the Constitution of the United States or the Constitution of North Carolina.

(9)   Subsequent admission of evidence from a witness when there has been an improperly overruled objection to the admission of evidence on the ground that the witness is for a specified reason incompetent or not qualified or disqualified.

(10)   Subsequent admission of evidence involving a specified line of questioning when there has been an improperly overruled objection to the admission of evidence involving that line of questioning.

61

(11)   Questions propounded to a witness by the court or a juror.

(12)   Rulings and orders of the court, not directed to the admissibility of evidence during trial, when there has been no opportunity to make an objection or motion.

(13)   Error of law in the charge to the jury.

(14)   The court has expressed to the jury an opinion as to whether a fact is fully or sufficiently proved.

(15)   The defendant was not present at any proceeding at which his presence was required.

(16)   Error occurred in the entry of the plea.

(17)   The form of the verdict was erroneous.

(18)   The sentence imposed was unauthorized at the time imposed, exceeded the maximum authorized by law, was illegally imposed, or is otherwise invalid as a matter of law.

(19)   A significant change in law, either substantive or procedural, applies to the proceedings leading to the defendant's conviction or sentence, and retroactive application of the changed legal standard is required. (1977, c. 711, s. 1; 1977, 2nd Sess., c. 1147, s. 28; 1983 (Reg. Sess., 1984), c. 1037, s. 1.)

§ 15A-1447. Relief available upon appeal.

(a)   If the appellate court finds that there has been reversible error which denied the defendant a fair trial conducted in accordance with law, it must grant the defendant a new trial.

(b)   If the appellate court finds that the facts charged in a pleading were not at the time charged a crime, the judgment must be reversed and the charge must be dismissed.

(c)   If the appellate court finds that the evidence with regard to a charge is insufficient as a matter of law, the judgment must be reversed and the charge must be dismissed unless there is evidence to support a lesser included offense. In that case the court may remand for trial on the lesser offense.

(d)   If the appellate court affirms only some of the charges, or if it finds error relating only to the sentence, it may direct the return of the case to the trial court for the imposition of an appropriate sentence.

(e)   If the appellate court affirms one or more of the charges, but not all of them, and makes a finding that the sentence is sustained by the charge or charges which are affirmed and is appropriate, the court may affirm the sentence.

(f)   If the appellate court finds that there is an error with regard to the sentence which may be corrected without returning the case to the trial division for that purpose, it may direct the entry of the appropriate sentence.

(g)   If the appellate court finds that there has been reversible error and the rule against double jeopardy prohibits further prosecution, it must dismiss the charges with prejudice. (1977, c. 711, s. 1.)

§ 15A-1448. Procedures for taking appeal.

(a)   Time for Entry of Appeal; Jurisdiction over the Case. -

(1)   A case remains open for the taking of an appeal to the appellate division for the period provided in the rules of appellate procedure for giving notice of appeal.

(2)   When a motion for appropriate relief is made under G.S. 15A-1414 or G.S. 15A-1416(a), the case remains open for the taking of an appeal until the court has ruled on the motion. The time for taking an appeal as provided in subsection (b) shall begin to run immediately upon the entry of an order under G.S. 15A-1420(c)(7), and the case shall remain open for the taking of an appeal until the expiration of that time.

(3)   The jurisdiction of the trial court with regard to the case is divested, except as to actions authorized by G.S. 15A-1453, when notice of appeal has been given and the period described in (1) and (2) has expired.

63

(4)   Repealed by Session Laws 1987, c. 624.

(5)   The right to appeal is not waived by withdrawal of an appeal if the appeal is reentered within the time specified in (1) and (2).

(6)   The right to appeal is not waived by compliance with all or a portion of the judgment imposed. If the defendant appeals, the court may enter appropriate orders remitting any fines or costs which have been paid. The court may delay the remission pending the determination of the appeal.

(b)   How and When Appeal of Right Taken. - Notice of appeal shall be given within the time, in the manner and with the effect provided in the rules of appellate procedure.

(c)   Certiorari. - Petitions for writs of certiorari are governed by rules of the appellate division. (1977, c. 711, s. 1; 1977, 2nd Sess., c. 1147, s. 29; 1987, c. 624; 1989, c. 377, s. 5.)

§ 15A-1449. Security for costs not required.

In criminal cases no security for costs is required upon appeal to the appellate division. (1977, c. 711, s. 1.)

§ 15A-1450. Withdrawal of appeal.

An appeal may be withdrawn by filing with the clerk of superior court a written notice of the withdrawal, signed by the defendant and, if he has counsel, his attorney. The clerk must forward a copy of the notice to the clerk of the appellate division in which the case is pending. The appellate division may enter an appropriate order with regard to the costs of the appeal. (1977, c. 711, s. 1.)

§ 15A-1451. Stay of sentence; bail; no stay when State appeals.

(a)   When a defendant has given notice of appeal:

(1)   Payment of costs is stayed.

(2)   Payment of a fine is stayed.

(3)   Confinement is stayed only when the defendant has been released pursuant to Article 26, Bail.

(4)   Probation or special probation is stayed.

(b)   The effect of dismissal of charges is not stayed by an appeal by the State, and the defendant is free from such charges unless they are subsequently reinstated as a result of the determination upon appeal. (1977, c. 711, s. 1.)

§ 15A-1452. Execution of sentence upon determination of appeal; compliance with directive of appellate court.

(a)   If an appeal is withdrawn, the clerk of superior court must enter an order reflecting that fact and directing compliance with the judgment.

(b)   If the appellate division affirms the judgment in whole or in part, the clerk of superior court must file the directive of the appellate division and order compliance with its terms.

(c)   If the appellate division orders a new trial or directs other relief or proceedings, the clerk must file the directive of the appellate court and bring the directive to the attention of the district attorney or the court for compliance with the directive. (1977, c. 711, s. 1.)

§ 15A-1453. Ancillary actions during appeal.

(a)   While an appeal is pending in the appellate division, the court in which the defendant was convicted has continuing authority to act with regard to the defendant's release pursuant to Article 26, Bail.

(b)   The appropriate court of the appellate division may direct that additional steps be taken in the trial court while the appeal is pending, including but not limited to:

(1)   Appointment of counsel.

(2)   Hearings with regard to matters relating to the appeal.

(3)   Taking evidence or conducting other proceedings relating to motions for appropriate relief made in the appellate division, as provided in G.S. 15A-1418. (1977, c. 711, s. 1.)

§ 15A-1454. Reserved for future codification purposes.

§ 15A-1455. Reserved for future codification purposes.

§ 15A-1456. Reserved for future codification purposes.

§ 15A-1457. Reserved for future codification purposes.

§ 15A-1458. Reserved for future codification purposes.

§ 15A-1459. Reserved for future codification purposes.

Article 92.

North Carolina Innocence Inquiry Commission.

§ 15A-1460. Definitions.

The following definitions apply in this Article:

(1)   "Claim of factual innocence" means a claim on behalf of a living person convicted of a felony in the General Court of Justice of the State of North Carolina, asserting the complete innocence of any criminal responsibility for the felony for which the person was convicted and for any other reduced level of criminal responsibility relating to the crime, and for which there is some credible, verifiable evidence of innocence that has not previously been presented at trial or considered at a hearing granted through postconviction relief.

(1a)   "Claimant" means a person asserting that he or she is completely innocent of any criminal responsibility for a felony crime upon which the person was convicted and for any other reduced level of criminal responsibility relating to the crime.

(2)   "Commission" means the North Carolina Innocence Inquiry Commission established by this Article.

(3)   "Director" means the Director of the North Carolina Innocence Inquiry Commission.

(4)   "Victim" means the victim of the crime, or if the victim of the crime is deceased, the next of kin of the victim. (2006-184, s. 1; 2010-171, s. 5; 2012-7, s. 4.)

§ 15A-1461. Purpose of Article.

This Article establishes an extraordinary procedure to investigate and determine credible claims of factual innocence that shall require an individual to voluntarily waive rights and privileges as described in this Article. (2006-184, s. 1; 2010-171, s. 5.)

§ 15A-1462. Commission established.

(a)   There is established the North Carolina Innocence Inquiry Commission. The North Carolina Innocence Inquiry Commission shall be an independent commission under the Judicial Department for administrative purposes.

(b)   The Administrative Office of the Courts shall provide administrative support to the Commission as needed. The Director of the Administrative Office of the Courts shall not reduce or modify the budget of the Commission or use funds appropriated to the Commission without the approval of the Commission. (2006-184, s. 1; 2010-171, s. 5.)

§ 15A-1463. Membership; chair; meetings; quorum.

(a)   The Commission shall consist of eight voting members as follows:

(1)   One shall be a superior court judge.

(2)   One shall be a prosecuting attorney.

(3)   One shall be a victim advocate.

(4)   One shall be engaged in the practice of criminal defense law.

(5)   One shall be a public member who is not an attorney and who is not an officer or employee of the Judicial Department.

(6)   One shall be a sheriff holding office at the time of his or her appointment.

(7)   The vocations of the two remaining appointed voting members shall be at the discretion of the Chief Justice.

The Chief Justice of the North Carolina Supreme Court shall make the initial appointment for members identified in subdivisions (4) through (6) of this subsection. The Chief Judge of the Court of Appeals shall make the initial appointment for members identified in subdivisions (1) through (3) of this subsection. After an appointee has served his or her first three-year term, the subsequent appointment shall be by the Chief Justice or Chief Judge who did not make the previous appointment. Thereafter, the Chief Justice or Chief Judge shall rotate the appointing power, except for the two discretionary appointments identified by subdivision (7) of this subsection which shall be appointed by the Chief Justice.

(b)   The appointing authority shall also appoint alternate Commission members for the Commission members he or she has appointed to serve in the event of scheduling conflicts, conflicts of interest, disability, or other disqualification arising in a particular case. The alternate members shall have the same qualifications for appointment as the original member. In making the appointments, the appointing authority shall make a good faith effort to appoint members with different perspectives of the justice system. The appointing authority shall also consider geographical location, gender, and racial diversity in making the appointments.

(c)   The superior court judge who is appointed as a member under subsection (a) of this section shall serve as Chair of the Commission. The Commission shall have its initial meeting no later than January 31, 2007, at the call of the Chair. The Commission shall meet a minimum of once every six months and may also meet more often at the call of the Chair. The Commission shall meet at such time and place as designated by the Chair. Notice of the meetings shall be given at such time and manner as provided by the rules of the Commission. A majority of the members shall constitute a quorum. All Commission votes shall be by majority vote. (2006-184, s. 1; 2010-171, s. 5.)

§ 15A-1464. Terms of members; compensation; expenses.

(a)   Of the initial members, two appointments shall be for one-year terms, three appointments shall be for two-year terms, and three appointments shall be for three-year terms. Thereafter, all terms shall be for three years. Members of the Commission shall serve no more than two consecutive three-year terms plus any initial term of less than three years. Unless provided otherwise by this act, all terms of members shall begin on January 1 and end on December 31.

Members serving by virtue of elective or appointive office, except for the sheriff, may serve only so long as the officeholders hold those respective offices. The Chief Justice may remove members, with cause. Vacancies occurring before the expiration of a term shall be filled in the manner provided for the members first appointed.

(b)   The Commission members shall receive no salary for serving. All Commission members shall receive necessary subsistence and travel expenses in accordance with the provisions of G.S. 138-5 and G.S. 138-6, as applicable. (2006-184, s. 1; 2010-171, s. 5.)

§ 15A-1465. Director and other staff.

(a)   The Commission shall employ a Director. The Director shall be an attorney licensed to practice in North Carolina at the time of appointment and at all times during service as Director. The Director shall assist the Commission in developing rules and standards for cases accepted for review, coordinate investigation of cases accepted for review, maintain records for all case investigations, prepare reports outlining Commission investigations and recommendations to the trial court, and apply for and accept on behalf of the Commission any funds that may become available from government grants, private gifts, donations, or devises from any source.

(b)   Subject to the approval of the Chair, the Director shall employ such other staff and shall contract for services as is necessary to assist the Commission in the performance of its duties, and as funds permit.

(c)   The Commission may, with the approval of the Legislative Services Commission, meet in the State Legislative Building or the Legislative Office Building, or may meet in an area provided by the Director of the Administrative Office of the Courts. The Director of the Administrative Office of the Courts shall provide office space for the Commission and the Commission staff. (2006-184, s. 1; 2010-171, s. 5; 2011-284, s. 11.)

§ 15A-1466. Duties.

The Commission shall have the following duties and powers:

(1)   To establish the criteria and screening process to be used to determine which cases shall be accepted for review.

(2)   To conduct inquiries into claims of factual innocence, with priority to be given to those cases in which the convicted person is currently incarcerated solely for the crime for which he or she claims factual innocence.

(3)   To coordinate the investigation of cases accepted for review.

(4)   To maintain records for all case investigations.

(5)   To prepare written reports outlining Commission investigations and recommendations to the trial court at the completion of each inquiry.

(6)   To apply for and accept any funds that may become available for the Commission's work from government grants, private gifts, donations, or devises from any source. (2006-184, s. 1; 2010-171, s. 5; 2011-284, s. 12.)

§ 15A-1467. Claims of innocence; waiver of convicted person's procedural safeguards and privileges; formal inquiry; notification of the crime victim.

(a)   A claim of factual innocence may be referred to the Commission by any court, a State or local agency, a claimant, or a claimant's counsel. The Commission shall not consider a claim of factual innocence if the convicted person is deceased. The determination of whether to grant a formal inquiry regarding any other claim of factual innocence is in the discretion of the Commission. The Commission may informally screen and dismiss a case summarily at its discretion.

(b)   No formal inquiry into a claim of innocence shall be made by the Commission unless the Director or the Director's designee first obtains a signed agreement from the convicted person in which the convicted person waives his or her procedural safeguards and privileges, agrees to cooperate with the Commission, and agrees to provide full disclosure regarding all inquiry requirements of the Commission. The waiver under this subsection does not apply to matters unrelated to a convicted person's claim of innocence. The convicted person shall have the right to advice of counsel prior to the execution of the agreement and, if a formal inquiry is granted, throughout the formal inquiry. If counsel represents the convicted person, then the convicted person's counsel must be present at the signing of the agreement. If counsel does not represent the convicted person, the Commission Chair shall determine the convicted person's indigency status and, if appropriate, enter an order for the appointment of counsel for the purpose of advising on the agreement.

(c)   If a formal inquiry regarding a claim of factual innocence is granted, the Director shall use all due diligence to notify the victim in the case and explain the inquiry process. The Commission shall give the victim notice that the victim has the right to present his or her views and concerns throughout the Commission's investigation.

(d)   The Commission may use any measure provided in Chapter 15A of the General Statutes and the Rules of Civil Procedure as set out in G.S. 1A-1 to obtain information necessary to its inquiry. The Commission may also do any of the following: issue process to compel the attendance of witnesses and the production of evidence, administer oaths, petition the Superior Court of Wake County or of the original jurisdiction for enforcement of process or for other relief, and prescribe its own rules of procedure. All challenges with regard to the Commission's authority or the Commission's access to evidence shall be heard by the Commission Chair in the Chair's judicial capacity, including any in camera review required by G.S. 15A-908.

(e)   While performing duties for the Commission, the Director or the Director's designee may serve subpoenas or other process issued by the Commission throughout the State in the same manner and with the same effect as an officer authorized to serve process of the General Court of Justice.

(f)   All State discovery and disclosure statutes in effect at the time of formal inquiry shall be enforceable as if the convicted person were currently being tried for the charge for which the convicted person is claiming innocence.

(g)   If, at any point during an inquiry, the convicted person refuses to comply with requests of the Commission or is otherwise deemed to be uncooperative by the Commission, the Commission shall discontinue the inquiry. (2006-184, s. 1; 2010-171, s. 5; 2012-7, s. 5.)

§ 15A-1468. Commission proceedings.

(a)   At the completion of a formal inquiry, all relevant evidence shall be presented to the full Commission. As part of its proceedings, the Commission may conduct public hearings. The determination as to whether to conduct public hearings is solely in the discretion of the Commission. Any public hearing held in accordance with this section shall be subject to the Commission's rules of operation.

(a1)   The Commission may compel the testimony of any witness. If a witness asserts his or her privilege against self-incrimination in a proceeding under this Article, the Commission chair, in the chair's judicial capacity, may order the witness to testify or produce other information if the chair first determines that the witness's testimony will likely be material to reach a correct factual determination in the case at hand. However, the Commission chair shall not order the witness to testify or produce other information that would incriminate the witness in the prosecution of any offense other than an offense for which the witness is granted immunity under this subsection. The order shall prevent a prosecutor from using the compelled testimony, or evidence derived therefrom, to prosecute the witness for previous false statements made under oath by the witness in prior proceedings. The prosecutor has a right to be heard by the Commission chair prior to the chair issuing the order. Once granted, the

72

immunity shall apply throughout all proceedings conducted pursuant to this Article. The limited immunity granted under this section shall not prohibit prosecution of statements made under oath that are unrelated to the Commission's formal inquiry, false statements made under oath during proceedings under this Article, or prosecution for any other crimes.

(a2)   The Innocence Inquiry Commission shall include, as part of its rules of operation, the holding of a prehearing conference to be held at least 10 days prior to any proceedings of the full Commission. Only the following persons shall be notified and authorized to attend the prehearing conference: the District Attorney, or the District Attorney's designee, of the district where the claimant was convicted of the felony upon which the claim of factual innocence is based; the claimant's counsel, if any; the Chair of the Commission; the Executive Director of the Commission; and any Commission staff designated by the Director. The District Attorney, or designee, shall be provided (i) an opportunity to inspect any evidence that may be presented to the Commission that has not previously been presented to any judicial officer or body and (ii) any information that he or she deems relevant to the proceedings. Prior to any Commission proceedings, the District Attorney or designee is authorized to provide the Commission with a written statement, which shall be included in the record of the Commission's proceedings. Any statement included in the record shall be part of the Commission's record of proceedings pursuant to subsection (e) of this section.

(b)   The Director shall use all due diligence to notify the victim at least 30 days prior to any proceedings of the full Commission held in regard to the victim's case. The Commission shall notify the victim that the victim is permitted to attend proceedings otherwise closed to the public, subject to any limitations imposed by this Article. If the victim plans to attend proceedings otherwise closed to the public, the victim shall notify the Commission at least 10 days in advance of the proceedings of his or her intent to attend.

(c)   After hearing the evidence, the full Commission shall vote to establish further case disposition as provided by this subsection. All eight voting members of the Commission shall participate in that vote.

Except in cases where the convicted person entered and was convicted on a plea of guilty, if five or more of the eight voting members of the Commission conclude there is sufficient evidence of factual innocence to merit judicial review, the case shall be referred to the senior resident superior court judge in the district of original jurisdiction by filing with the clerk of court the opinion of the

73

Commission with supporting findings of fact, as well as the record in support of such opinion, with service on the district attorney in noncapital cases and service on both the district attorney and Attorney General in capital cases. In cases where the convicted person entered and was convicted on a plea of guilty, if all of the eight voting members of the Commission conclude there is sufficient evidence of factual innocence to merit judicial review, the case shall be referred to the senior resident superior court judge in the district of original jurisdiction.

If less than five of the eight voting members of the Commission, or in cases where the convicted person entered and was convicted on a guilty plea less than all of the eight voting members of the Commission, conclude there is sufficient evidence of factual innocence to merit judicial review, the Commission shall conclude there is insufficient evidence of factual innocence to merit judicial review. The Commission shall document that opinion, along with supporting findings of fact, and file those documents and supporting materials with the clerk of superior court in the district of original jurisdiction, with a copy to the district attorney and the senior resident superior court judge.

The Director of the Commission shall use all due diligence to notify immediately the victim of the Commission's conclusion in a case.

(d)   Evidence of criminal acts, professional misconduct, or other wrongdoing disclosed through formal inquiry or Commission proceedings shall be referred to the appropriate authority. Evidence favorable to the convicted person disclosed through formal inquiry or Commission proceedings shall be disclosed to the convicted person and the convicted person's counsel, if the convicted person has counsel.

(e)   All proceedings of the Commission shall be recorded and transcribed as part of the record. All Commission member votes shall be recorded in the record. All records and proceedings of the Commission are confidential and are exempt from public record and public meeting laws except that the supporting records for the Commission's conclusion that there is sufficient evidence of factual innocence to merit judicial review, including all files and materials considered by the Commission and a full transcript of the hearing before the Commission, shall become public at the time of referral to the superior court. Commission records for conclusions of insufficient evidence of factual innocence to merit judicial review shall remain confidential, except as provided in subsection (d) of this section. (2006-184, s. 1; 2009-360, s. 1; 2010-171, s. 5; 2012-7, ss. 6, 7.)

74

§ 15A-1469. Postcommission three-judge panel.

(a)   If the Commission concludes there is sufficient evidence of factual innocence to merit judicial review, the Chair of the Commission shall request the Chief Justice to appoint a three-judge panel, not to include any trial judge that has had substantial previous involvement in the case, and issue commissions to the members of the three-judge panel to convene a special session of the superior court of the original jurisdiction to hear evidence relevant to the Commission's recommendation. The senior judge of the panel shall preside. The Chief Justice shall appoint the three-judge panel within 20 days of the filing of the Commission's opinion finding sufficient evidence of factual innocence to merit judicial review.

(a1)   If the Commission concludes that there is credible evidence of prosecutorial misconduct in the case, the Chair of the Commission may request the Attorney General to appoint a special prosecutor to represent the State in lieu of the district attorney of the district of conviction or the district attorney's designee. The request for the special prosecutor shall be made within 20 days of the filing of the Commission's opinion finding sufficient evidence of innocence to merit judicial review.

Upon receipt of a request under this subsection to appoint a special prosecutor, the Attorney General may temporarily assign a district attorney, assistant district attorney, or other qualified attorney, to represent the State at the hearing before the three-judge panel. However, the Attorney General shall not appoint as special prosecutor any attorney who prosecuted or assisted with the prosecution in the trial of the convicted person, or is a prosecuting attorney in the district where the convicted person was tried. The appointment shall be made no later than 20 days after the receipt of the request.

(b)   The senior resident superior court judge shall enter an order setting the case for hearing at the special session of superior court for which the three-judge panel is commissioned and shall require the State to file a response to the Commission's opinion within 90 days of the date of the order. Such response, at the time of original filing or through amendment at any time before or during the proceedings, may include joining the defense in a motion to dismiss the charges with prejudice on the basis of innocence.

(c)   The district attorney of the district of conviction, or the district attorney's designee, shall represent the State at the hearing before the three-judge panel, except as otherwise provided by this section.

(d)   The three-judge panel shall conduct an evidentiary hearing. At the hearing, the court, and the defense and prosecution through the court, may compel the testimony of any witness, including the convicted person. All credible, verifiable evidence relevant to the case, even if considered by a jury or judge in a prior proceeding, may be presented during the hearing. The convicted person may not assert any privilege or prevent a witness from testifying. The convicted person has a right to be present at the evidentiary hearing and to be represented by counsel. A waiver of the right to be present shall be in writing.

(e)   The senior resident superior court judge shall determine the convicted person's indigency status and, if appropriate, enter an order for the appointment of counsel. The court may also enter an order relieving an indigent convicted person of all or a portion of the costs of the proceedings.

(f)   The clerk of court shall provide written notification to the victim 30 days prior to any case-related hearings.

(g)   Upon the motion of either party, the senior judge of the panel may direct the attorneys for the parties to appear before him or her for a conference on any matter in the case.

(h)   The three-judge panel shall rule as to whether the convicted person has proved by clear and convincing evidence that the convicted person is innocent of the charges. Such a determination shall require a unanimous vote. If the vote is unanimous, the panel shall enter dismissal of all or any of the charges. If the vote is not unanimous, the panel shall deny relief.

(i)   A person who is determined by the three-judge panel to be innocent of all charges and against whom the charges are dismissed pursuant to this section is eligible for compensation under Article 8 of Chapter 148 of the General Statutes without obtaining a pardon of innocence from the Governor. (2006-184, s. 1; 2010-171, ss. 1, 5; 2012-7, s. 8.)

§ 15A-1470. No right to further review of decision by Commission or three-judge panel; convicted person retains right to other postconviction relief.

(a)   Unless otherwise authorized by this Article, the decisions of the Commission and of the three-judge panel are final and are not subject to further review by appeal, certification, writ, motion, or otherwise.

76

(b)   A claim of factual innocence asserted through the Innocence Inquiry Commission shall not adversely affect the convicted person's rights to other postconviction relief. (2006-184, s. 1; 2010-171, s. 5.)

§ 15A-1471. Preservation of files and evidence; production of files and evidence; forensic and DNA testing.

(a)   Upon receiving written notice from the Commission of a Commission inquiry, the State shall preserve all files and evidence subject to disclosure under G.S. 15A-903. Once the Commission provides written notice to the State that the Commission's inquiry is complete, the duty to preserve under this section shall cease; however, other preservation requirements may be applicable.

(b)   The Commission is entitled to a copy of all records preserved under subsection (a) of this section, including access to inspect and examine all physical evidence.

(c)   Upon request of the Commission, the State shall transfer custody of physical evidence to the Commission's Director, or the Director's designee, for forensic and DNA testing. The Commission shall preserve evidence in a manner reasonably calculated to prevent contamination or degradation of any biological evidence that might be present, while subject to a continuous chain of custody and securely retained with sufficient official documentation to locate the evidence. At or prior to the completion of the Commission's inquiry, the Commission shall return all remaining evidence.

(d)   The Commission shall have the right to subject physical evidence to forensic and DNA testing, including consumption of biological material, as necessary for the Commission's inquiry. If testing complies with FBI requirements and the data meets NDIS criteria, profiles obtained from the testing shall be searched and uploaded to CODIS. The Commission shall incur all costs associated with ensuring compliance with FBI requirements and NDIS criteria. (2012-7, s. 10.)

§ 15A-1472. Reserved for future codification purposes.

§ 15A-1473. Reserved for future codification purposes.

§ 15A-1474. Reserved for future codification purposes.

§ 15A-1475. Reports.

Beginning January 1, 2008, and annually thereafter, the North Carolina Innocence Inquiry Commission shall report on its activities to the Joint Legislative Oversight Committee on Justice and Public Safety and the State Judicial Council. The report may contain recommendations of any needed legislative changes related to the activities of the Commission. The report shall recommend the funding needed by the Commission, the district attorneys, and the State Bureau of Investigation in order to meet their responsibilities under S.L. 2006-184. Recommendations concerning the district attorneys or the State Bureau of Investigation shall only be made after consultations with the North Carolina Conference of District Attorneys and the Attorney General. (2006-184, s. 9; 2011-291, s. 2.4.)

Articles 93 to 99.

§§ 15A-1476 through 15A-1999. Reserved for future codification purposes.

SUBCHAPTER XV. CAPITAL PUNISHMENT.

Article 100.

Capital Punishment.

§ 15A-2000. Sentence of death or life imprisonment for capital felonies; further proceedings to determine sentence.

(a)   Separate Proceedings on Issue of Penalty. -

(1)   Except as provided in G.S. 15A-2004, upon conviction or adjudication of guilt of a defendant of a capital felony in which the State has given notice of its intent to seek the death penalty, the court shall conduct a separate sentencing proceeding to determine whether the defendant should be sentenced to death or life imprisonment. A capital felony is one which may be punishable by death.

(2)   The proceeding shall be conducted by the trial judge before the trial jury as soon as practicable after the guilty verdict is returned. If prior to the time that the trial jury begins its deliberations on the issue of penalty, any juror dies, becomes incapacitated or disqualified, or is discharged for any reason, an alternate juror shall become a part of the jury and serve in all respects as those selected on the regular trial panel. An alternate juror shall become a part of the jury in the order in which he was selected. If the trial jury is unable to reconvene for a hearing on the issue of penalty after having determined the guilt of the accused, the trial judge shall impanel a new jury to determine the issue of the punishment. If the defendant pleads guilty, the sentencing proceeding shall be conducted before a jury impaneled for that purpose. A jury selected for the purpose of determining punishment in a capital case shall be selected in the same manner as juries are selected for the trial of capital cases.

(3)   In the proceeding there shall not be any requirement to resubmit evidence presented during the guilt determination phase of the case, unless a new jury is impaneled, but all such evidence is competent for the jury's consideration in passing on punishment. Evidence may be presented as to any matter that the court deems relevant to sentence, and may include matters relating to any of the aggravating or mitigating circumstances enumerated in subsections (e) and (f) of this section. Any evidence which the court deems to have probative value may be received.

(4)   The State and the defendant or his counsel shall be permitted to present argument for or against sentence of death. The defendant or defendant's counsel shall have the right to the last argument.

(b)   Sentence Recommendation by the Jury. - Instructions determined by the trial judge to be warranted by the evidence shall be given by the court in its charge to the jury prior to its deliberation in determining sentence. The court shall give appropriate instructions in those cases in which evidence of the defendant's mental retardation requires the consideration by the jury of the provisions of G.S. 15A-2005. In all cases in which the death penalty may be authorized, the judge shall include in his instructions to the jury that it must consider any aggravating circumstance or circumstances or mitigating circumstance or circumstances from the lists provided in subsections (e) and (f) which may be supported by the evidence, and shall furnish to the jury a written list of issues relating to such aggravating or mitigating circumstance or circumstances.

After hearing the evidence, argument of counsel, and instructions of the court, the jury shall deliberate and render a sentence recommendation to the court, based upon the following matters:

(1)   Whether any sufficient aggravating circumstance or circumstances as enumerated in subsection (e) exist;

(2)   Whether any sufficient mitigating circumstance or circumstances as enumerated in subsection (f), which outweigh the aggravating circumstance or circumstances found, exist; and

(3)   Based on these considerations, whether the defendant should be sentenced to death or to imprisonment in the State's prison for life.

The sentence recommendation must be agreed upon by a unanimous vote of the 12 jurors. Upon delivery of the sentence recommendation by the foreman of the jury, the jury shall be individually polled to establish whether each juror concurs and agrees to the sentence recommendation returned.

If the jury cannot, within a reasonable time, unanimously agree to its sentence recommendation, the judge shall impose a sentence of life imprisonment; provided, however, that the judge shall in no instance impose the death penalty when the jury cannot agree unanimously to its sentence recommendation.

(c)   Findings in Support of Sentence of Death. - When the jury recommends a sentence of death, the foreman of the jury shall sign a writing on behalf of the jury which writing shall show:

(1)   The statutory aggravating circumstance or circumstances which the jury finds beyond a reasonable doubt; and

(2)   That the statutory aggravating circumstance or circumstances found by the jury are sufficiently substantial to call for the imposition of the death penalty; and,

(3)   That the mitigating circumstance or circumstances are insufficient to outweigh the aggravating circumstance or circumstances found.

(d)   Review of Judgment and Sentence. -

(1)   The judgment of conviction and sentence of death shall be subject to automatic review by the Supreme Court of North Carolina pursuant to procedures established by the Rules of Appellate Procedure. In its review, the Supreme Court shall consider the punishment imposed as well as any errors assigned on appeal.

(2)   The sentence of death shall be overturned and a sentence of life imprisonment imposed in lieu thereof by the Supreme Court upon a finding that the record does not support the jury's findings of any aggravating circumstance or circumstances upon which the sentencing court based its sentence of death, or upon a finding that the sentence of death was imposed under the influence of passion, prejudice, or any other arbitrary factor, or upon a finding that the sentence of death is excessive or disproportionate to the penalty imposed in similar cases, considering both the crime and the defendant. The Supreme Court may suspend consideration of death penalty cases until such time as the court determines it is prepared to make the comparisons required under the provisions of this section.

(3)   If the sentence of death and the judgment of the trial court are reversed on appeal for error in the post-verdict sentencing proceeding, the Supreme Court shall order that a new sentencing hearing be conducted in conformity with the procedures of this Article.

(e)   Aggravating Circumstances. - Aggravating circumstances which may be considered shall be limited to the following:

(1)   The capital felony was committed by a person lawfully incarcerated.

(2)   The defendant had been previously convicted of another capital felony or had been previously adjudicated delinquent in a juvenile proceeding for committing an offense that would be a capital felony if committed by an adult.

(3)   The defendant had been previously convicted of a felony involving the use or threat of violence to the person or had been previously adjudicated delinquent in a juvenile proceeding for committing an offense that would be a Class A, B1, B2, C, D, or E felony involving the use or threat of violence to the person if the offense had been committed by an adult.

(4)   The capital felony was committed for the purpose of avoiding or preventing a lawful arrest or effecting an escape from custody.

(5)   The capital felony was committed while the defendant was engaged, or was an aider or abettor, in the commission of, or an attempt to commit, or flight after committing or attempting to commit, any homicide, robbery, rape or a sex offense, arson, burglary, kidnapping, or aircraft piracy or the unlawful throwing, placing, or discharging of a destructive device or bomb.

(6)   The capital felony was committed for pecuniary gain.

(7)   The capital felony was committed to disrupt or hinder the lawful exercise of any governmental function or the enforcement of laws.

(8)   The capital felony was committed against a law-enforcement officer, employee of the Division of Adult Correction of the Department of Public Safety, jailer, fireman, judge or justice, former judge or justice, prosecutor or former prosecutor, juror or former juror, or witness or former witness against the defendant, while engaged in the performance of his official duties or because of the exercise of his official duty.

(9)   The capital felony was especially heinous, atrocious, or cruel.

(10)   The defendant knowingly created a great risk of death to more than one person by means of a weapon or device which would normally be hazardous to the lives of more than one person.

(11)   The murder for which the defendant stands convicted was part of a course of conduct in which the defendant engaged and which included the commission by the defendant of other crimes of violence against another person or persons.

(f)   Mitigating Circumstances. - Mitigating circumstances which may be considered shall include, but not be limited to, the following:

(1)   The defendant has no significant history of prior criminal activity.

(2)   The capital felony was committed while the defendant was under the influence of mental or emotional disturbance.

(3)   The victim was a voluntary participant in the defendant's homicidal conduct or consented to the homicidal act.

(4)   The defendant was an accomplice in or accessory to the capital felony committed by another person and his participation was relatively minor.

(5)   The defendant acted under duress or under the domination of another person.

(6)   The capacity of the defendant to appreciate the criminality of his conduct or to conform his conduct to the requirements of law was impaired.

(7)   The age of the defendant at the time of the crime.

(8)   The defendant aided in the apprehension of another capital felon or testified truthfully on behalf of the prosecution in another prosecution of a felony.

(9)   Any other circumstance arising from the evidence which the jury deems to have mitigating value. (1977, c. 406, s. 2; 1979, c. 565, s. 1; c. 682, s. 9; 1981, c. 652, s. 1; 1994, Ex. Sess., c. 7, s. 5; 1995, c. 509, s. 14; 2001-81, s. 1; 2001-346, s. 2; 2011-145, s. 19.1(h).)

§ 15A-2001. Capital offenses; plea of guilty.

(a)   Any defendant who has been indicted for an offense punishable by death may enter a plea of guilty at any time after the indictment.

(b)   If the defendant enters a guilty plea to first degree murder and the State has not given notice of intent to seek the death penalty as provided in G.S. 15A-2004 or the State has agreed to accept a sentence of life imprisonment where it initially gave notice of intent to seek the death penalty, then the court shall sentence the person to life imprisonment. The defendant may plead guilty to first degree murder and the State may agree to accept a sentence of life imprisonment, even if evidence of an aggravating circumstance exists.

(c)   If the defendant enters a guilty plea to first degree murder and the State has given notice of its intent to seek the death penalty, then the court may sentence the defendant to life imprisonment or to death pursuant to the procedures of G.S. 15A-2000. Before sentencing the defendant in a case in which the State has given notice of its intent to seek the death penalty, the presiding judge shall impanel a jury for the limited purpose of hearing evidence and determining a sentence recommendation as to the appropriate sentence pursuant to G.S. 15A-2000. The jury's sentence recommendation in cases where the defendant pleads guilty and the State has given notice of its intent to seek the death penalty shall be determined under the same procedure of G.S. 15A-2000 applicable to defendants who have been tried and found guilty by a jury. (1977, c. 406, s. 2; 2001-81, s. 2.)

§ 15A-2002. Capital offenses; jury verdict and sentence.

If the recommendation of the jury is that the defendant be sentenced to death, the judge shall impose a sentence of death in accordance with the provisions of Chapter 15, Article 19 of the General Statutes. If the recommendation of the jury is that the defendant be imprisoned for life in the State's prison, the judge shall impose a sentence of imprisonment for life in the State's prison, without parole.

The judge shall instruct the jury, in words substantially equivalent to those of this section, that a sentence of life imprisonment means a sentence of life without parole. (1977, c. 406, s. 2; 1993, c. 538, s. 29; 1994, Ex. Sess., c. 21, s. 5; c. 24, s. 14(b).)

§ 15A-2003. Disability of trial judge.

In the event that the trial judge shall become disabled or unable to conduct the sentencing proceeding provided in this Article, the Chief Justice shall designate a judge to conduct such proceeding. (1977, c. 406, s. 2.)

§ 15A-2004. Prosecutorial discretion.

(a)   The State, in its discretion, may elect to try a defendant capitally or noncapitally for first degree murder, even if evidence of an aggravating circumstance exists. The State may agree to accept a sentence of life imprisonment for a defendant at any point in the prosecution of a capital felony, even if evidence of an aggravating circumstance exists.

84

(b)   A sentence of death may not be imposed upon a defendant convicted of a capital felony unless the State has given notice of its intent to seek the death penalty. Notice of intent to seek the death penalty shall be given to the defendant and filed with the court on or before the date of the pretrial conference in capital cases required by Rule 24 of the General Rules of Practice for the Superior and District Courts, or the arraignment, whichever is later. A court may discipline or sanction the State for failure to comply with the time requirements in Rule 24, but shall not declare a case as noncapital as a consequence of such failure. In addition to any discipline or sanctions the court may impose, the court shall continue the case for a sufficient time so that the defendant is not prejudiced by any delays in holding the hearing required by Rule 24.

(c)   If the State has not given notice of its intent to seek the death penalty prior to trial, the trial shall be conducted as a noncapital proceeding, and the court, upon adjudication of the defendant's guilt of first degree murder, shall impose a sentence of life imprisonment.

(d)   Notwithstanding any other provision of Article 100 of Chapter 15A of the General Statutes, the State may agree to accept a sentence of life imprisonment for a defendant upon remand from the Supreme Court of North Carolina of a capital case for resentencing or upon an order of resentencing by a court in a State or federal post-conviction proceeding. If the State exercises its discretion and does agree to accept a sentence of life imprisonment for the defendant, then the court shall impose a sentence of life imprisonment. (2001-81, s. 3; 2012-136, s. 2.)

§ 15A-2005. Mentally retarded defendants; death sentence prohibited.

(a)   (1)   The following definitions apply in this section:

a.   Mentally retarded. - Significantly subaverage general intellectual functioning, existing concurrently with significant limitations in adaptive functioning, both of which were manifested before the age of 18.

b.   Significant limitations in adaptive functioning. - Significant limitations in two or more of the following adaptive skill areas: communication, self-care, home living, social skills, community use, self-direction, health and safety, functional academics, leisure skills and work skills.

c.   Significantly subaverage general intellectual functioning. - An intelligence quotient of 70 or below.

(2)   The defendant has the burden of proving significantly subaverage general intellectual functioning, significant limitations in adaptive functioning, and that mental retardation was manifested before the age of 18. An intelligence quotient of 70 or below on an individually administered, scientifically recognized standardized intelligence quotient test administered by a licensed psychiatrist or psychologist is evidence of significantly subaverage general intellectual functioning; however, it is not sufficient, without evidence of significant limitations in adaptive functioning and without evidence of manifestation before the age of 18, to establish that the defendant is mentally retarded.

(b)   Notwithstanding any provision of law to the contrary, no defendant who is mentally retarded shall be sentenced to death.

(c)   Upon motion of the defendant, supported by appropriate affidavits, the court may order a pretrial hearing to determine if the defendant is mentally retarded. The court shall order such a hearing with the consent of the State. The defendant has the burden of production and persuasion to demonstrate mental retardation by clear and convincing evidence. If the court determines the defendant to be mentally retarded, the court shall declare the case noncapital, and the State may not seek the death penalty against the defendant.

(d)   The pretrial determination of the court shall not preclude the defendant from raising any legal defense during the trial.

(e)   If the court does not find the defendant to be mentally retarded in the pretrial proceeding, upon the introduction of evidence of the defendant's mental retardation during the sentencing hearing, the court shall submit a special issue to the jury as to whether the defendant is mentally retarded as defined in this section. This special issue shall be considered and answered by the jury prior to the consideration of aggravating or mitigating factors and the determination of sentence. If the jury determines the defendant to be mentally retarded, the court shall declare the case noncapital and the defendant shall be sentenced to life imprisonment.

(f)   The defendant has the burden of production and persuasion to demonstrate mental retardation to the jury by a preponderance of the evidence.

86

(g)   If the jury determines that the defendant is not mentally retarded as defined by this section, the jury may consider any evidence of mental retardation presented during the sentencing hearing when determining aggravating or mitigating factors and the defendant's sentence.

(h)   The provisions of this section do not preclude the sentencing of a mentally retarded offender to any other sentence authorized by G.S. 14-17 for the crime of murder in the first degree. (2001-346, s. 1.)

§ 15A-2006: Expired pursuant to Session Laws 2001-346, s. 3, effective October 1, 2002.

§ 15A-2007: Reserved for future codification purposes.

§ 15A-2008: Reserved for future codification purposes.

§ 15A-2009: Reserved for future codification purposes.

Article 101.

North Carolina Racial Justice Act.

§§ 15A-2010 through 15A-2012: Repealed by Session Laws 2013-154, s. 5(a), effective June 19, 2013

§§ 15A-2010 through 15A-2012: Repealed by Session Laws 2013-154, s. 5(a), effective June 19, 2013

Chapter 15B.

Victims Compensation.

Article 1.

Crime Victim's Compensation Act.

§ 15B-1. Short title.

This Article may be cited as the "North Carolina Crime Victims Compensation Act." (1983, c. 832, s. 1; 1991, c. 301, s. 1; 2004-159, s. 1.)

§ 15B-2. Definitions.

As used in this Article, the following definitions apply, unless the context requires otherwise:

(1)   Allowable expense. - Reasonable charges incurred for reasonably needed products, services, and accommodations, including those for medical care, rehabilitation, medically-related property, and other remedial treatment and care.

Allowable expense includes a total charge not in excess of five thousand dollars ($5,000) for expenses related to funeral, cremation, and burial, including transportation of a body, but excluding expenses for flowers, gravestone, and other items not directly related to the funeral service.

Allowable expense for medical care, counseling, rehabilitation, medically-related property, and other remedial treatment and care of a victim shall be limited to sixty-six and two-thirds percent (66 2/3%) of the amount usually charged by the provider for the treatment or care. By accepting the compensation paid as allowable expense pursuant to this subdivision, the provider agrees that the compensation is payment in full for the treatment or care and shall not charge or otherwise hold a claimant financially responsible for the cost of services in addition to the amount of allowable expense.

(2)   Claimant. - Any of the following persons who claims an award of compensation under this Article:

a.   A victim;

b.   A dependent of a deceased victim;

c.   A third person who is not a collateral source and who provided benefit to the victim or his family other than in the course or scope of his employment, business, or profession;

88

d.   A person who is authorized to act on behalf of a victim, a dependent, or a third person described in sub-subdivision c. of this subdivision;

e.   A person who was convicted of a first offense under G.S. 14-204 and whose participation in the offense was a result of having been a trafficking victim under G.S. 14-43.11 or G.S. 14-43.13 or a victim of a severe form of trafficking under the federal Trafficking Victims Protection Act (22 U.S.C. § 7102(13)).

The claimant, however, may not be the offender or an accomplice of the offender who committed the criminally injurious conduct, except as provided in sub-subdivision e. of this subdivision.

(3)   Collateral source. - A source of benefits or advantages for economic loss otherwise compensable that the victim or claimant has received or that is readily available to the victim or the claimant from any of the following sources:

a.   The offender.

b.   The government of the United States or any of its agencies, a state or any of its political subdivisions, or an instrumentality of two or more states.

c.   Social Security, Medicare, or Medicaid.

d.   State-required, temporary, nonoccupational disability insurance.

e.   Worker's compensation.

f.   Wage continuation programs of any employer.

g.   Proceeds of a contract of insurance payable to the victim for loss that the victim sustained because of the criminally injurious conduct.

h.   A contract providing prepaid hospital and other health care services, or benefits for disability.

i.   A contract of insurance that will pay for expenses directly related to a funeral, cremation, and burial, including transportation of a body.

j.   A charitable gift or donation by a third party, including a charity care write-off of expenses by a medical provider, regardless of whether the gift or donation is subsequently rescinded.

(4)   Commission. - The Crime Victims Compensation Commission established by G.S. 15B-3.

(4a)   Consumer reporting agency. - As defined in G.S. 75-61(4).

(4b)   Credit report. - As defined in G.S. 75-61(3).

(5)   Criminally injurious conduct. - Conduct that by its nature poses a substantial threat of personal injury or death, and is punishable by fine or imprisonment or death, or would be so punishable but for the fact that the person engaging in the conduct lacked the capacity to commit the crime under the laws of this State. Criminally injurious conduct includes conduct that amounts to an offense involving impaired driving as defined in G.S. 20-4.01(24a), and conduct that amounts to a violation of G.S. 20-166 if the victim was a pedestrian or was operating a vehicle moved solely by human power or a mobility impairment device. For purposes of this Article, a mobility impairment device is a device that is designed for and intended to be used as a means of transportation for a person with a mobility impairment, is suitable for use both inside and outside a building, and whose maximum speed does not exceed 12 miles per hour when the device is being operated by a person with a mobility impairment. Criminally injurious conduct does not include conduct arising out of the ownership, maintenance, or use of a motor vehicle when the conduct is punishable only as a violation of other provisions of Chapter 20 of the General Statutes. Criminally injurious conduct shall also include an act of terrorism, as defined in 18 U.S.C. § 2331, that is committed outside of the United States against a citizen of this State.

(6)   Dependent. - An individual wholly or substantially dependent upon the victim for care and support and includes a child of the victim born after his death.

(7)   Dependent's economic loss. - Loss after a victim's death of contributions of things of economic value to his dependents, not including services they would have received from the victim if he had not suffered the fatal injury, less expenses of the dependents avoided by reason of the victim's death. Dependent's economic loss will be limited to a 26-week period commencing from the date of the injury, and compensation shall not exceed three hundred dollars ($300.00) per week.

(8)   Dependent's replacement service loss. - Loss reasonably incurred by dependents after a victim's death in obtaining ordinary and necessary services

in lieu of those the victim would have performed for their benefit if he had not suffered the fatal injury, less expenses of the dependents avoided by reason of the victim's death and not subtracted in calculating dependent's economic loss.

Dependent's replacement service loss will be limited to a 26-week period commencing from the date of the injury and compensation shall not exceed two hundred dollars ($200.00) per week.

(9)   Director. - The Director of the Commission appointed under G.S. 15B-3(g).

(10)   Economic loss. - Economic detriment consisting only of allowable expense, work loss, replacement services loss, and household support loss. If criminally injurious conduct causes death, economic loss includes a dependent's economic loss and a dependent's replacement service loss. Noneconomic detriment is not economic loss, but economic loss may be caused by pain and suffering or physical impairment.

(10a)   Household support loss. - The loss of support that a victim would have received from the victim's spouse for the purpose of maintaining a home or residence for the victim and the victim's dependents. A victim may be compensated fifty dollars ($50.00) per week for each dependent child. Compensation for household support loss shall not exceed three hundred dollars ($300.00) per week and shall be limited to 26 weeks commencing from the date of the injury. A victim may receive only one compensation for household support loss. Household support loss is only available to an unemployed victim whose spouse is the offender who committed the criminally injurious conduct that is the basis of the victim's claim under this act.

(11)   Noneconomic detriment. - Pain, suffering, inconvenience, physical impairment, or other nonpecuniary damage.

(12)   Replacement services loss. - Expenses reasonably incurred in obtaining ordinary and necessary services in lieu of those the injured person would have performed, not for income but for the benefit of himself or his family, if he had not been injured.

Replacement service loss will be limited to a 26-week period commencing from the date of the injury, and compensation may not exceed two hundred dollars ($200.00) per week.

91

(12a) Substantial evidence. - Relevant evidence that a reasonable mind might accept as adequate to support a conclusion.

(13) Victim. - A person who suffers personal injury or death proximately caused by criminally injurious conduct.

(14) Work loss. - Loss of income from work that the injured person would have performed if he had not been injured and expenses reasonably incurred by him to obtain services in lieu of those he would have performed for income, reduced by any income from substitute work actually performed by him, or by income he would have earned in available appropriate substitute work that he was capable of performing but unreasonably failed to undertake.

Compensation for work loss will be limited to 26 weeks commencing from the date of the injury, and compensation shall not exceed three hundred dollars ($300.00) per week. A claim for work loss will be paid only upon proof that the injured person was gainfully employed at the time of the criminally injurious conduct and, by physician's certificate, that the injured person was unable to work. (1983, c. 832, s. 1; 1987, c. 819, ss. 1-8; 1989, c. 322, s. 1; c. 679, s. 1; 1991, c. 301, s. 1; 1997-227, ss. 1, 2; 1998-212, s. 19.4(l); 2004-124, s. 18.1; 2004-159, s. 1; 2006-183, ss. 1, 2; 2009-355, s. 5; 2011-267, s. 1; 2013-368, s. 15.)

§ 15B-3. Crime Victims Compensation Commission.

(a)   There is established the Crime Victims Compensation Commission of the Department of Public Safety, consisting of seven members as follows:

(1)   One member to be appointed by the Governor;

(2)   One member to be appointed by the General Assembly upon the recommendation of the President Pro Tempore of the Senate under G.S. 120-121;

(3)   One member to be appointed by the General Assembly upon the recommendation of the Speaker of the House of Representatives under G.S. 120-121;

(4)   The Attorney General or the Attorney General's designee;

(5)   The Secretary of the Department of Public Safety or the Secretary's designee; and

(6)   Two members to be appointed by the Secretary of the Department of Public Safety.

(b)   Members shall serve terms of four years. A member shall continue to serve until his successor is duly appointed, but a holdover under this provision does not affect the expiration date of the succeeding term.

(c)   In case of a vacancy on the Commission before the expiration of a member's term, a successor shall be appointed within 30 days of the vacancy for the remainder of the unexpired term by the appropriate official pursuant to subsection (a). Vacancies in legislative appointments shall be filled under G.S. 120-122.

(d)   The Commission shall elect one of its members as chairman to serve until the expiration of his term.

(e)   A majority of the Commission constitutes a quorum to transact business.

(f)   Members shall receive compensation and reimbursement for expenses as provided in G.S. 138-5.

(g)   The Commission shall name a Director upon the recommendation of the Secretary of Public Safety. The Director shall serve at the pleasure of the Commission. The Department of Public Safety shall provide for the compensation of the Director and shall provide professional and clerical staff necessary for the work of the Commission. (1983, c. 832, s. 1; 1987, c. 819, ss. 9, 10; 1991, c. 301, s. 1; 1995, c. 490, s. 14; 1999-269, s. 1; 2004-159, s. 1; 2011-145, s. 19.1(g).)

§ 15B-4. Award of compensation.

(a)   Subject to the limitations in G.S. 15B-22, compensation for criminally injurious conduct shall be awarded to a claimant if substantial evidence establishes that the requirements for an award have been met. Compensation shall only be paid for economic loss and not for noneconomic detriment. The

Commission shall follow the rules of liability applicable to civil tort law in North Carolina.

(b)   Compensation shall only be awarded for criminally injurious conduct that occurs or is attempted in this State except that criminally injurious conduct that occurs or is attempted against a resident of this State while in another state which does not have a victims compensation program of any type may be a basis of compensation. (1983, c. 832, s. 1; 1987, c. 819, s. 11; 1989, c. 322, s. 2; 1991, c. 301, s. 1; 2004-159, s. 1; 2006-183, s. 3.)

§ 15B-5. Attorney General to represent State.

The Attorney General shall represent the interest of the State when:

(1)   A decision of the Commission is appealed to the courts; and

(2)   When the State is sued or when it brings or enters a lawsuit pursuant to this Article. (1983, c. 832, s. 1; 1991, c. 301, s. 1; 2004-159, s. 1.)

§ 15B-6. Powers of the Commission and Director.

(a)   In addition to powers authorized by this Article and Chapter 150B, the Commission may:

(1)   Adopt rules in accordance with Part 3, Article 1 of Chapter 143B and Article 2A of Chapter 150B of the General Statutes necessary to carry out the purposes of this Article;

(2)   Establish general policies and guidelines for awarding compensation and provide guidance to the staff assigned by the Secretary of the Department of Public Safety to administer the program;

(3)   Accept for any lawful purpose and functions under this Article any and all donations, both real and personal, and grants of money from any governmental unit or public agency, or from any institution, person, firm, or corporation, and may deposit the same to the Crime Victims Compensation Fund.

(b)   The Director shall have the following authority:

(1)   With the consent of the district attorney, to request that law enforcement officers employed by the State or any political subdivision provide copies of any information or data gathered in the investigation of criminally injurious conduct that is the basis of any claim to enable the Director or Commission to determine whether, and the extent to which, a claimant qualifies for an award of compensation;

(2)   With the consent of the district attorney, to request that prosecuting attorneys, law enforcement officers, and State agencies conduct investigations and provide information necessary to enable the Director or Commission to determine whether, and the extent to which, a claimant qualifies for an award of compensation; and

(3)   To require the claimant to supplement the application for an award of compensation with any reasonably available medical or psychological reports pertaining to the injury for which the award of compensation is claimed.

Information obtained pursuant to this subsection is subject to the same privilege against public disclosure that may be asserted by the providing source. (1983, c. 832, s. 1; 1987, c. 819, s. 12; 1989, c. 679, s. 2; 1991, c. 301, s. 1; 2000-189, s. 3; 2004-159, s. 1; 2011-145, s. 19.1(g).)

§ 15B-7. Filing of application for compensation award; contents.

(a)   A claim for an award of compensation is commenced by filing an application for an award with the Director. The application shall be in a form prescribed by the Commission and shall contain the following information:

(1)   The name and address of the victim of the criminally injurious conduct, the name and address of the claimant, and the relationship of the claimant to the victim;

(2)   If the victim is deceased, the name and address of each dependent of the victim and the extent to which each is dependent upon the victim for care and support;

(3)   The nature of the criminally injurious conduct that is the basis for the claim and the date on which the conduct occurred;

(4)   The law-enforcement agency or officer to whom the criminally injurious conduct was reported and the date on which it was reported;

(5)   The nature and extent of the injuries that the victim sustained from the criminally injurious conduct for which compensation is sought, the name and address of any person who gave medical treatment to the victim for the injuries, the name and address of any hospital or similar institution where the victim received medical treatment for the injuries, and whether the victim died as a result of the injuries;

(6)   The total amount of the economic loss that the victim, a dependent, or the claimant sustained as a result of the criminally injurious conduct, without regard to the financial limitations set forth in G.S. 15B-11(f) and (g).

(7)   The amount of benefits or advantages that the victim, a dependent, or other claimant has received or is entitled to receive from any collateral source for economic loss that resulted from the criminally injurious conduct, and the name of each collateral source;

(8)   Whether the claimant is the spouse, parent, child, brother, or sister of the offender, or is similarly related to an accomplice of the offender who committed the criminally injurious conduct;

(9)   A release authorizing the Commission and the Commission's staff to obtain any report, document, or information that relates to the determination of the claim for an award of compensation;

(10)   Any additional relevant information that the Commission may require. The Commission may require the claimant to submit, with the application, materials to substantiate the facts that are stated in the application.

(b)   A person who knowingly and willfully presents or attempts to present a false or fraudulent application, or a State officer or employee who knowingly and willfully participates or assists in the preparation or presentation of a false or fraudulent application is guilty of a Class 1 misdemeanor if the application is for a claim of not more than four hundred dollars ($400.00). If the application is for a claim of more than four hundred dollars ($400.00), the person is guilty of a

Class I felony. (1983, c. 832, s. 1; 1987, c. 819, s. 13; 1991, c. 301; 1993, c. 539, s. 303; 1994, Ex. Sess., c. 24, s. 14(c).)

§ 15B-8. Procedure for filing application.

(a)   The Director shall establish procedures for screening, filing, recording, investigating, and processing applications for an award of compensation. The Director shall also establish the procedures and methods for processing follow-up claims for compensation. The procedures and methods established by the Director under this subsection shall conform to any rules adopted by the Commission.

(b)   Repealed by Session Laws 1987, c. 819, s. 14. (1983, c. 832, s. 1; 1987, c. 819, s. 14; 1991, c. 301, s. 1.)

§ 15B-8.1. Privilege and records of the Commission.

(a)   In a proceeding under this Article, the privileges set forth in G.S. 8-53, 8-53.3, 8-53.4, 8-53.7, 8-53.8, and 8-56 do not apply to communications or records concerning the physical, mental or emotional condition of the claimant or victim if that condition is relevant to a claim for compensation.

(b)   All medical information relating to the mental, physical, or emotional condition of a victim or claimant and all law enforcement records and information and any juvenile records shall be held confidential by the Commission and Director. All personal information, as that term is defined in 18 U.S.C. § 2725(3), of victims and claimants and all information concerning the disposition of claims for compensation, except for the total amount awarded a victim or claimant, shall be held confidential by the Commission and Director. Except for information held confidential under this subsection, the records of the Division shall be open to public inspection. (1989, c. 679, s. 3; 2004-159, s. 1; 2011-267, s. 2.)

§ 15B-9. Repealed by Session Laws 1987, c. 819, s. 15, effective August 13, 1987.

97

§ 15B-10. Awarding claims.

(a)   The Director shall decide the award of compensation for an initial claim or follow-up claim when the claim does not exceed twelve thousand five hundred dollars ($12,500) and does not include future economic loss. The Director shall report all awards under this subsection to the Commission.

(b)   The Director shall recommend the award of compensation for an initial claim or follow-up claim when the claim exceeds twelve thousand five hundred dollars ($12,500) or involves future economic loss. The Commission shall decide the award of compensation for a claim based on a review of written evidence submitted to the Commission by the Director.

(c)   In reporting a decision under subsection (a) or recommending a decision under subsection (b), the Director shall submit to the Commission documentation to establish the economic loss of the claimant by substantial evidence.

(d)   The Director shall send each claimant a written statement of a decision made under subsection (a) or (b) that gives the reasons for the decision. A claimant who is dissatisfied with a decision may commence a contested case under Article 3 of Chapter 150B of the General Statutes. (1983, c. 832, s. 1; 1987, c. 819, s. 16; 1991, c. 301, s. 1; 1999-269, s. 2; 2004-159, s. 1; 2009-354, s. 3.)

§ 15B-11. Grounds for denial of claim or reduction of award.

(a)   An award of compensation shall be denied if:

(1)   The claimant fails to file an application for an award within two years after the date of the criminally injurious conduct that caused the injury or death for which the claimant seeks the award;

(2)   The economic loss is incurred after one year from the date of the criminally injurious conduct that caused the injury or death for which the victim seeks the award, except in the case where the victim for whom compensation is sought was 10 years old or younger at the time the injury occurred. In that case an award of compensation will be denied if the economic loss is incurred after

two years from the date of the criminally injurious conduct that caused the injury or death for which the victim seeks the award;

(3)   The criminally injurious conduct was not reported to a law enforcement officer or agency within 72 hours of its occurrence, and there was no good cause for the delay;

(4)   The award would benefit the offender or the offender's accomplice, unless a determination is made that the interests of justice require that an award be approved in a particular case;

(5)   The criminally injurious conduct occurred while the victim was confined in any State, county, or city prison, correctional, youth services, or juvenile facility, or local confinement facility, or half-way house, group home, or similar facility; or

(6)   The victim was participating in a felony at or about the time that the victim's injury occurred.

(b)   A claim may be denied or an award of compensation may be reduced if:

(1)   The victim was participating in a nontraffic misdemeanor at or about the time that the victim's injury occurred; or

(2)   The claimant or a victim through whom the claimant claims engaged in contributory misconduct.

(b1)   The Commission or Director, whichever has the authority to decide a claim under G.S. 15B-10, shall exercise discretion in determining whether to deny a claim under subsection (b) of this section. In exercising discretion, the Commission or Director shall consider whether any proximate cause exists between the injury and the misdemeanor or contributory misconduct, when applicable. The Director or Commission shall deny claims upon a finding that there was contributory misconduct that is a proximate cause of becoming a victim. However, contributory misconduct that is not a proximate cause of becoming a victim shall not lead to an automatic denial of a claim.

(c)   A claim may be denied, an award of compensation may be reduced, and a claim that has already been decided may be reconsidered upon finding that the claimant or victim, without good cause, has not fully cooperated with appropriate law enforcement agencies or in the prosecution of criminal cases with regard to the criminally injurious conduct that is the basis for the award.

(c1)   A claim may be denied upon a finding that the claimant has been convicted of any felony classified as a Class A, B1, B2, C, D, or E felony under the laws of the State of North Carolina and that such felony was committed within 3 years of the time the victim's injury occurred.

(d)   After reaching a decision to approve an award of compensation, but before notifying the claimant, the Director shall require the claimant to submit current information as to collateral sources on forms prescribed by the Commission.

An award that has been approved shall nevertheless be denied or reduced to the extent that the economic loss upon which the claim is based is or will be recouped from a collateral source. If an award is reduced or a claim is denied because of the expected recoupment of all or part of the economic loss of the claimant from a collateral source, the amount of the award or the denial of the claim shall be conditioned upon the claimant's economic loss being recouped by the collateral source. If it is thereafter determined that the claimant will not receive all or part of the expected recoupment, the claim shall be reopened and an award shall be approved in an amount equal to the amount of expected recoupment that it is determined the claimant will not receive from the collateral source, subject to the limitations set forth in subsections (f) and (g).

(e)   Repealed by Session Laws 1998-212, s. 19.4(m), effective December 1, 1998.

(f)   Repealed by Session Laws 2011-267, s. 3, effective July 1, 2011.

(g)   Compensation payable to a victim and to all other claimants sustaining economic loss because of injury to, or the death of, that victim may not exceed thirty thousand dollars ($30,000) in the aggregate in addition to allowable funeral, cremation, and burial expenses.

(h)   The right to reconsider or reopen a claim does not affect the finality of its decision for the purpose of judicial review. (1983, c. 832, s. 1; 1987, c. 819, ss. 17-21; 1989 (Reg. Sess., 1990), c. 898, s. 1; c. 1066, s. 131; 1991, c. 301, s. 1; 1994, Ex. Sess., c. 3, s. 1; 1997-227, s. 3; 1998-212, s. 19.4(m); 1999-269, s. 3; 2004-159, s. 1; 2006-183, ss. 4, 5; 2009-354, s. 4; 2011-267, s. 3; 2011-326, s. 3.)

100

§ 15B-12. Evidence in contested cases.

(a)   Except as provided in this section, evidence in a contested case shall be taken in accordance with Article 3 of Chapter 150B of the General Statutes.

(b)   In a proceeding under this Article, the privileges set forth in G.S. 8-53, 8-53.3, 8-53.4, 8-53.7, 8-53.8, and 8-56 do not apply to communications or records concerning the physical, mental or emotional condition of the claimant or victim if that condition is relevant to a claim for compensation.

(c)   If the mental, physical, or emotional condition of a victim or claimant is material to a claim for an award of compensation, the administrative law judge may order the victim or claimant to submit to a mental or physical examination by a physician or psychologist, and may order an autopsy of a deceased victim. The order may be made for good cause shown and upon notice to the person to be examined and to the claimant. The order shall specify the time, place, manner, conditions, and scope of the examination or autopsy and the person by whom it is to be made, and shall require the person who performs the examination or autopsy to file with the administrative law judge a detailed written report of the examination or autopsy. The report shall set out the findings, including the results of all tests made, diagnosis, prognosis, and other conclusions, and reports of earlier examinations of the same conditions. On request of the person examined, the administrative law judge shall furnish him a copy of the report. If the victim is deceased, the administrative law judge on request, shall furnish the claimant a copy of the report.

(d)   The administrative law judge may request that law-enforcement officers employed by the State or any political subdivision thereof provide it with copies of any information or data gathered in the investigation of the criminally injurious conduct that is the basis of any claim to enable it to determine whether, and the extent to which, a claimant qualifies for an award of compensation. The administrative law judge may also request that prosecuting attorneys, law-enforcement officers, and State agencies conduct investigations and provide information necessary to enable the administrative law judge to determine whether, and the extent to which, a claimant qualifies for an award of compensation. Information obtained pursuant to this subsection is subject to the same privilege against public disclosure that may be asserted by the providing source.

(e)   The administrative law judge may require the claimant to supplement the application for an award of compensation with any reasonably available medical or psychological reports relating to the injury for which the award of compensation is claimed.

(f)   The administrative law judge may not request the victim or the claimant to supply any evidence that would not be admissible at a trial under G.S. 8C-1, Rule 412.

(g)   Notwithstanding any provision to the contrary relating to the confidentiality of juvenile records, the administrative law judge shall have access to the records of juvenile proceedings which bear upon an application for compensation, but to the extent possible, it shall maintain the confidentiality of those records.

(h)   The administrative law judge may exclude from a hearing of any matter at issue all persons, except those engaged in the hearing, during the taking of medical information and law-enforcement investigative records and information as evidence.

(i)   Except for information held confidential by the administrative law judge, the official record in a contested case under this Article is open to public inspection. (1983, c. 832, s. 1; 1987, c. 819, s. 22; 1989, c. 679, ss. 4, 5; 1991, c. 301, s. 1; 2004-159, s. 1.)

§ 15B-13. Repealed by Session Laws 1987, c. 819, s. 23.

§ 15B-14. Effect of prosecution or conviction of offender.

(a)   An award of compensation may be approved whether or not any person is prosecuted or convicted for committing the conduct that is the basis of the award. Proof of conviction of a person whose conduct gave rise to a claim is conclusive evidence that the crime was committed, unless an application for rehearing, an appeal of the conviction, or a writ of certiorari is pending, or a rehearing or new trial has been ordered.

(b)   Upon a request of the Attorney General, the proceedings in a claim for an award of compensation shall be suspended pending disposition of a criminal prosecution that has been commenced or is imminent.

(c)   In making an award, any specific statement of loss to a victim that a trial court has included in its judgment in the case may be considered. (1983, c. 832, s. 1; 1987, c. 819, s. 24; 1991, c. 301, s. 1; 2004-159, s. 1; 2011-267, s. 4.)

§ 15B-15. Clerks of court to be notified.

The Director shall notify in writing the clerk of superior court of the county in which the offense occurred of any award made from the Crime Victims Compensation Fund to the victim. The clerk shall place the notice in the case file of any defendant charged with the offense that gave rise to the award to the victim. (1983, c. 832, s. 1; 1987, c. 819, s. 25; 1991, c. 301, s. 1.)

§ 15B-16. Manner of payment; non-assignability and exemptions.

(a)   The Director shall pay award payments directly to the service provider on behalf of the claimant. Eligible out-of-pocket costs borne by the claimant shall be paid directly to the victim only if such costs can be documented and verified.

(b)   Upon request of the claimant, future economic loss, other than allowable expense, may be commuted to a lump sum only on a finding that:

(1)   The award in a lump sum will promote the interests of the claimant; or

(2)   The present value of all future economic loss other than allowable expense does not exceed one thousand dollars ($1,000).

(c)   An award for future economic loss payable in installments may be made only for a period as to which future economic loss can reasonably be determined. An award for future economic loss payable in installments may be reconsidered and modified upon a finding that a material and substantial change of circumstances has occurred.

(d)   An order on reconsideration of an award may not require refund of amounts previously paid unless the award was obtained by fraud.

(e)   The Director, even after an award made by the Commission, may negotiate with any service provider in order to obtain a reduction of the amount claimed by the provider in exchange for a full release of any claim against a claimant. (1983, c. 832, s. 1; 1987, c. 819, s. 26; 1989, c. 679, s. 6; 1991, c. 301, s. 1; 2004-159, s.1.)

§ 15B-17. Award not subject to taxation or execution.

(a)   An award is exempt from taxation.

(b)   An award is not subject to execution, attachment, garnishment, or other process, except that, upon receipt of an award by a claimant, the part of the award that is for allowable expense is not exempt from such an action by a creditor to the extent that he provides products, services, or accommodations the costs of which are included in the award, and the part of the award that is for work loss is not exempt from such an action to secure payment of alimony, maintenance, or child support. (1983, c. 832, s. 1; 1991, c. 301, s. 1.)

§ 15B-18. Subrogation by State.

(a)   If compensation is awarded, the Crime Victims Compensation Fund is subrogated to all the claimant's rights to receive or recover benefits or advantages for economic loss from a source that is, or if readily available to the victim or claimant would be, a collateral source, to the extent of the compensation awarded.

(b)   The Crime Victims Compensation Fund is an eligible recipient for restitution under G.S. 15A-1021, 15A-1343, 148-33.1, 148-33.2, 148-57.1, and any other applicable statutes.

(c)   As a prerequisite to bringing an action to recover damages related to criminally injurious conduct for which compensation is claimed or awarded, the claimant shall give the Commission prior written notice of the proposed action. After receiving the notice the Commission shall immediately notify the Attorney General who shall promptly:

(1)   Join in the action as a party plaintiff to recover compensation awarded;

104

(2)   Require that the claimant bring the action in his individual name as a trustee in behalf of the State to recover compensation awarded; or

(3)   Reserve its rights and do neither in the proposed action. If, as requested by the Attorney General, the claimant brings the action as trustee and recovers compensation awarded from the Crime Victims Compensation Fund, he may deduct from the compensation recovered in behalf of the State the reasonable expenses, including attorney fees, allocable by the court for that recovery.

(d)   If a judgment or verdict separately indicates economic loss and noneconomic detriment, payments on the judgment shall be allocated between them in proportion to the amounts indicated. In an action in a court of this State arising out of criminally injurious conduct, the judge, on timely motion, shall direct the jury to return a special verdict, indicating separately the awards for noneconomic detriment, punitive damages, and economic loss.

(e)   Any funds recovered by the Crime Victims Compensation Fund pursuant to this section shall be paid to the general fund.

(f)   The Director may pursue any claim of the Crime Victim's Compensation Fund or the Commission set forth in this Article. At the request of the Director, or otherwise, the Attorney General is authorized to assert the rights of the Crime Victim's Compensation Fund or Commission before any administrative or judicial tribunal for purposes of enforcing a claim or right set forth in this Article. (1983, c. 832, s. 1; 1987, c. 819, s. 27; 1989, c. 679, s. 6; 1991, c. 301, s. 1; 2004-159, s. 1.)

§ 15B-19. Subrogation by collateral sources prohibited.

Subrogation rights that a collateral source may have may not extend to a recovery from a claimant of all or any part of an award made under this Article. A collateral source may not apply in the name of a claimant or otherwise for an award of compensation based upon injury to a claimant to whose rights the collateral source may be subrogated. (1983, c. 832, s. 1; 1991, c. 301, s. 1; 2004-159, s. 1.)

§ 15B-20. Publicity.

Law enforcement agencies responsible for investigating offenses committed in the State may provide information to victims of those offenses and to their dependents concerning the existence of the Crime Victims Compensation Fund and the source of applications for compensation from the Fund. (1983, c. 832, s. 1; 1987, c. 819, s. 28; 1991, c. 301, s. 1.)

§ 15B-21. Annual report.

The Commission shall, by March 15 each year, prepare and transmit to the Governor and the General Assembly a report of its activities in the prior fiscal year and the current fiscal year to date. The report shall include:

(1)   The number of claims filed;

(2)   The number of awards made;

(2a)   The number of pending cases by year received;

(3)   The amount of each award;

(4)   A statistical summary of claims denied and awards made;

(5)   The administrative costs of the Commission, including the compensation of commissioners;

(6)   The current unencumbered balance of the North Carolina Crime Victims Compensation Fund;

(7)   The amount of funds carried over from the prior fiscal year;

(8)   The amount of funds received in the prior fiscal year from the Division of Adult Correction of the Department of Public Safety and from the compensation fund established pursuant to the Victims Crime Act of 1984, 42 U.S.C. § 10601, et seq.; and

(9)   The amount of funds expected to be received in the current fiscal year, as well as the amount actually received in the current fiscal year on the date of the report, from the Division of Adult Correction of the Department of Public

106

Safety and from the compensation fund established pursuant to the Victims Crime Act of 1984, 42 U.S.C. § 10601, et seq.

The Attorney General and State Auditor shall assist the Commission in the preparation of the report required by this section. (1983, c. 832, s. 1; 1987, c. 819, s. 29; 1991, c. 301, s. 1; 1999-237, s. 20.2; 2001-424, s. 26.5; 2004-159, s. 1; 2011-145, s. 19.1(h).)

§ 15B-22. Disbursements.

If compensation awarded under this Article cannot be paid due to insufficient funds in the Crime Victims Compensation Fund, payment shall be delayed until sufficient funds are available and no further awards of compensation shall be made until sufficient funds are available. (1983, c. 832, s. 1; 1987, c. 819, s. 31; 1991, c. 301, s. 1; 2004-159, s. 1.)

§ 15B-23. Crime Victims Compensation Fund.

There is established the Crime Victims Compensation Fund. Revenue in the Crime Victims Compensation Fund includes amounts credited to the Fund under G.S. 148-2 and other funds. Any surplus in the Crime Victims Compensation Fund shall not revert. The Crime Victims Compensation Fund shall be kept on deposit with the State Treasurer, as in the case of other State funds, and may be invested by the State Treasurer in any lawful security for the investment of State money. The Crime Victims Compensation Fund is subject to the oversight of the State Auditor pursuant to Article 5A of Chapter 147 of the General Statutes. (1987, c. 819, s. 30; 1993 (Reg. Sess., 1994), c. 769, s. 21.5(b); 2004-159, s. 1.)

§ 15B-24. Requiring defendant to pay restitution encouraged.

Pursuant to a Court's power to require restitution as a condition of probation, parole or work-release privileges, a Court may require a defendant to pay restitution to a victim, regardless of whether the victim receives compensation from the Crime Victims Compensation Fund, or to the Fund. It is the intent of the

General Assembly that a victim's receipt of compensation from the Fund shall not discourage a Court from considering, where appropriate, payment of restitution by the defendant and alternatives to incarceration of the defendant. (1987, C. 819, S. 33.)

§ 15B-25. Compensation limits.

This Article shall not be construed to create a right to receive compensation. Compensation payable under Chapter 15B shall only be available to the extent that the General Assembly appropriates funds that purpose. (1987, c. 819, s. 36; 2004-159, s. 1.)

§ 15B-26. Crime victims credit protection.

(a)   A creditor that is owed money for services provided to a victim as a result of the criminally injurious conduct inflicted on the victim shall not communicate any information about the debt to a consumer reporting agency during the pendency of an application for an award filed pursuant to G.S. 15B-7 or during the pendency of an appeal from a decision related to such an application.

(b)   The victim bears the burden of notifying the creditor that the debt is subject to subsection (a) of this section.

(c)   A creditor may request monthly verification from the Commission that the application or appeal is still pending, and the Commission shall provide this verification. (2009-355, s. 6.)

§ 15B-27: Reserved for future codification purposes.

§ 15B-28: Reserved for future codification purposes.

§ 15B-29: Reserved for future codification purposes.

Article 2.

108

The Crime Victims Financial Recovery Assistance Act.

§ 15B-30. Declaration of policy and purpose.

The General Assembly of North Carolina hereby declares as a matter of public policy that:

(1)   No person who commits a crime should thereafter gain monetary profit as the result of committing the crime.

(2)   Victims of crime have a special relationship to any profit from the crime committed against them, including the personal belongings and memorabilia of a convicted felon whose criminal actions and resulting notoriety enhance the value of those belongings and memorabilia.

(3)   To the extent profit from crime would not have been realized but for an offender's commission of illegal acts, an offender does not have an equitable interest in the profit and allowing the offender to retain the profit would result in the offender's unjust enrichment.

The General Assembly finds that the State has a compelling interest in ensuring that persons convicted of crimes do not profit from those crimes, and that victims of crime are compensated by those who have harmed them.

The General Assembly further finds that crime victims have difficulty satisfying restitution orders or civil judgments entered against their offenders because the victims often lack the expertise and resources to identify or locate assets that an offender may have.

In order to carry out this public policy and to satisfy these compelling interests, the General Assembly has enacted the provisions of this Article providing a mechanism by which crime victims are notified of the existence of an offender's assets and are authorized to bring an action to recover those assets. (2004-159, s. 2.)

§ 15B-31. Definitions.

The following definitions apply in this Article:

(1)   Commission. - The Crime Victims Compensation Commission established under G.S. 15B-3.

(2)   Convicted. - A finding or verdict of guilty by a jury or by entry of a plea of guilty or no contest, or a finding of not guilty by reason of insanity.

(3)   Crime memorabilia. - Any tangible property belonging to or that belonged to an offender prior to conviction, the value of which is increased by the notoriety gained from the conviction of a felony.

(4)   Earned income. - Income derived from one's own labor or through active participation in a business, as distinguished from income including dividends or investments.

(5)   Eligible person. - Any of the following:

a.   A victim of the crime for which the offender was convicted.

b.   A surviving spouse, parent, or child of a deceased victim of the crime for which the offender was convicted.

c.   Any other person dependent for the person's principal support upon a deceased victim of the crime for which the offender was convicted.

However, "eligible person" does not include the offender or an accomplice to the offender.

(6)   Felony. - An offense defined as a felony by any North Carolina or United States statute that was committed in North Carolina and that resulted in physical or emotional injury, or death, to another person.

(7)   Funds of an offender. - All funds and property received from any source by an offender, excluding child support and earned income, where the offender:

a.   Is an inmate serving a sentence with the Division of Adult Correction of the Department of Public Safety or a prisoner confined at a local correctional facility or federal correctional institute, and includes funds that a superintendent, sheriff, or municipal official receives on behalf of an inmate or prisoner and deposits in an inmate account to the credit of the inmate or deposits in a prisoner account to the credit of the prisoner; or

b.   Is not an inmate or prisoner but who is serving a sentence of probation, conditional discharge, or post-release supervision.

(8)   Offender. - A person who has been convicted of a felony or that person's legal representative or assignee.

(9)   Profit from crime. - Any income, assets, or property obtained through or generated from the commission of a crime for which the offender was convicted, including any income, assets, or property generated from the sale of crime memorabilia or obtained through the use of unique knowledge obtained during the commission of, or in preparation for the commission of the crime, as well as any gain from the sale, conversion, or exchange of the income, assets, or property. "Profit from crime" does not include voluntary donations or contributions to an offender used to assist in the appeal of a conviction, provided the donation or contribution is not given in exchange for something of material value.

(10)   Victim. - Any natural person who suffers physical or emotional injury, or the threat of physical or emotional injury, as the result of the commission of a felony. (2004-159, s. 2; 2011-145, s. 19.1(h).)

§ 15B-32. Notice of contract or agreement to pay.

(a)   Notice to Commission. -

(1)   Every person, firm, corporation, partnership, association, or other legal entity, or representative of a person, firm, corporation, partnership, association, or entity that knowingly contracts for, pays, or agrees to pay to an offender (i) profit from crime or (ii) funds of an offender where the value or aggregate value of the payment or payments exceeds ten thousand dollars ($10,000) shall submit to the Commission a copy of the contract or reduce to writing the terms of any oral agreement or obligation to pay as soon as practicable after discovering the payment or intended payment constitutes profit from crime or funds of an offender.

(2)   Whenever the payment or obligation to pay involves funds of an offender that a superintendent, sheriff, or municipal officer (i) receives or will receive on behalf of an inmate serving a sentence with the Division of Adult Correction of the Department of Public Safety or a prisoner confined at a local

correctional facility, (ii) deposits or will deposit in an inmate account to the credit of an inmate or prisoner, and (iii) the value of such funds exceeds or will exceed ten thousand dollars ($10,000), the State or subdivision of the State shall also give written notice to the Commission.

(3)   Whenever the State or a subdivision of the State makes a payment or has an obligation to pay funds of an offender and the value of such funds exceeds or will exceed ten thousand dollars ($10,000), the State or subdivision of the State shall also give written notice to the Commission.

(4)   In all other instances where the payment or obligation to pay involves funds of an offender and the value or aggregate value of the funds exceeds or will exceed ten thousand dollars ($10,000), the offender who receives or will receive the funds shall give written notice to the Commission.

(b)   Notice to Eligible Persons. - The Commission shall, upon receipt of a notice of a contract, an agreement to pay, or payment of profit from crime or funds of an offender, notify in writing by certified mail, return receipt requested, all known eligible persons where the eligible persons' names and addresses are known to the Commission. The Commission may, in its discretion, provide for additional notice as it deems necessary. (2004-159, s. 2; 2011-145, s. 19.1(h).)

§ 15B-33. Penalties.

(a)   Assessment and Civil Penalty for Failure to Give Notice. - Any person or entity, other than the State, a subdivision of the State, or a person who is a superintendent, sheriff, or municipal official, who willfully fails to give notice as required by G.S. 15B-32 is subject to an assessment of up to the amount of the payment or obligation to pay and a civil penalty of up to one thousand dollars ($1,000) or ten percent (10%) of the payment or obligation to pay, whichever is greater.

(b)   Notice and Opportunity to Be Heard Required. - After providing notice and opportunity to be heard in accordance with the provisions of Chapter 150B of the General Statutes, the Commission may order the respondent to pay the assessment and civil penalty imposed by this section.

(c)   Failure to Pay. - If a respondent fails to pay the assessment and civil penalty imposed by this section within sixty (60) days of being ordered to pay, the assessment and civil penalty may be recovered from the respondent by an action brought by the attorney general, upon the request of the Commission, in any court of competent jurisdiction.

(d)   Establishment of Escrow Account; Notice to Eligible Persons. - The Commission shall deposit the assessment in an escrow account pending the expiration of the three-year statute of limitations authorized by G.S. 15B-34 to preserve the funds to satisfy a civil judgment in favor of an eligible person to whom the failure to give notice relates. The Commission shall notify any eligible person who may have a claim against the offender of the existence of the funds being held in escrow. The notice shall instruct the eligible person that the person may have a right to commence a civil action against the offender as well as any other information deemed necessary by the Commission.

(e)   Satisfaction of Judgment from Escrow Account. - Upon an eligible person's presentation to the Commission of a civil judgment for damages arising out of the offense for which the offender was convicted, the Commission shall satisfy up to one hundred percent (100%) of that judgment, including costs and disbursements as taxed by the clerk of the court, with the escrowed fund obtained pursuant to this section, but in no event shall the amount of all judgments, costs, and disbursements satisfied from the escrowed funds exceed the amount in escrow. If more than one eligible person indicates to the Commission that the eligible person intends to commence or has commenced a civil action against the offender, the Commission shall delay satisfying any judgment, costs, and disbursements until the claims of all eligible persons are reduced to judgment. If the aggregate of all judgments, costs, and disbursement obtained exceeds the amount of escrowed funds, the amount used to partially satisfy each judgment shall be reduced to a pro rata share.

(f)   Return of Unclaimed Escrowed Funds. - After the expiration of the three-year statute of limitations period established in G.S. 15B-34, the Commission shall review all judgments that have been satisfied from the escrowed funds. In the event no claim was filed prior to the expiration of the three-year statute of limitations, the Commission shall return the escrowed amount to the respondent. In the event a claim or claims are pending at the expiration of the statute of limitations, the funds shall remain escrowed until the final determination of all claims to allow the Commission to satisfy any judgment which may be obtained by the eligible person after which time any remaining escrowed amount shall be returned to the respondent.

113

(g)   Remittance of Proceeds from Civil Penalty. - The Commission shall remit the clear proceeds of the civil penalty of up to one thousand dollars ($1,000) or ten percent (10%) of the payment or obligation to pay, whichever is greater, assessed under this section to the Civil Penalty and Forfeiture Fund in accordance with G.S. 115C-457.2. (2004-159, s. 2.)

§ 15B-34. Civil action to recover profits or funds; responsibilities of the Commission.

(a)   Civil Action. - Notwithstanding any inconsistent provision of law with respect to the timely bringing of an action, an eligible person may, within three years of the discovery of any profit from crime or funds of an offender, bring a civil action in a court of competent jurisdiction against an offender for damages arising out of the offense for which the offender was convicted.

(b)   Notice by Eligible Persons. - Upon filing an action under subsection (a) of this section, the eligible person shall give notice to the Commission of the filing by delivering a copy of the summons and complaint to the Commission. The eligible person may also give notice to the Commission prior to filing the action so as to allow the Commission to apply for any appropriate provisional remedies, which are otherwise authorized to be invoked prior to the commencement of an action.

(c)   Responsibilities of Commission. - Upon receipt of a copy of a summons and complaint, or upon receipt of notice from the eligible person prior to filing an action, the Commission shall immediately take action to:

(1)   Notify all other known eligible persons of the filing of the civil action by certified mail, return receipt requested, where the eligible persons' names and addresses are known to the Commission.

(2)   Provide, in its discretion, for additional notice as it deems necessary.

(3)   Avoid the wasting of the assets identified in the complaint as the profit from crime or funds of an offender in any manner consistent with subsection (d) of this section.

(d)   Standing; Authority to Avoid Wasting of Assets. - The Commission has standing and, acting on its own behalf or on behalf of all eligible persons, shall

114

have the right to apply for any and all provisional remedies that are also otherwise available to the plaintiff in the civil action brought under subsection (a) of this section, including attachment, injunction, constructive trust, and receivership. On a motion for a provisional remedy, the moving party shall state whether any other provisional remedy has previously been sought in the same action against the same defendant. The court may require the moving party to elect between those remedies to which it would otherwise be entitled. (2004-159, s. 2.)

§ 15B-35. Subrogation by the Crime Victims Compensation Fund.

Claims on profit from crime or funds of an offender are subject to subrogation by the Crime Victims Compensation Fund pursuant to G.S. 15B-18. (2004-159, s. 2.)

§ 15B-36. Conviction overturned or pardon issued.

If profit from crime is subject to a provisional remedy on behalf of eligible persons and the conviction for the criminal offense from which profit from crime is realized is reversed, vacated, or set aside, or if the offender has been granted an unconditional pardon of innocence for the criminal offense, those funds shall be returned to the rightful owner. (2004-159, s. 2.)

§ 15B-37. Evasive action void.

Any action taken by an offender, whether by way of execution of a power of attorney, creation of corporate entities, or otherwise, to defeat the purpose of this Article shall be void as against the public policy of this State. (2004-159, s. 2.)

Chapter 15C.

Address Confidentiality Program.

§ 15C-1. Purpose.

The purpose of this Chapter is to enable the State and the agencies of North Carolina to respond to requests for public records without disclosing the location of a victim of domestic violence, sexual offense, stalking, or human trafficking; to enable interagency cooperation in providing address confidentiality for victims of domestic violence, sexual offense, stalking, or human trafficking; and to enable the State and its agencies to accept a program participant's use of an address designated by the Office of the Attorney General as a substitute address. (2002-171, s. 1; 2007-547, s. 4.)

§ 15C-2. Definitions.

The following definitions apply in this Chapter:

(1)   Actual address or address. - A residential, work, or school street address as specified on the individual's application to be a program participant under this Chapter.

(2)   Address Confidentiality Program or Program. - A program in the Office of the Attorney General to protect the confidentiality of the address of a relocated victim of domestic violence, sexual offense, or stalking to prevent the victim's assailants or potential assailants from finding the victim through public records.

(3)   Agency of North Carolina or agency. - Includes every elected or appointed State or local public office, public officer, or official; institution, board, commission, bureau, council, department, authority, or other unit of government of the State or of any local government; or unit, special district, or other political subdivision of State or local government.

(4)   Application assistant. - An employee of an agency or nonprofit organization who provides counseling, referral, shelter, or other specialized services to victims of domestic violence, sexual offense, stalking, or human trafficking and who has been designated by the Attorney General to assist individuals with applications to participate in the Address Confidentiality Program.

(5)   Attorney General. - Office of the Attorney General.

116

(6)   Person. - Any individual, corporation, limited liability company, partnership, trust, estate, or other association or any state, the United States, or any subdivision thereof.

(7)   Program participant. - An individual accepted into the Address Confidentiality Program in accordance with this Chapter.

(8)   Public record. - A public record as defined in Chapter 132 of the General Statutes.

(9)   Substitute address. - An address designated by the Attorney General under the Address Confidentiality Program.

(10)   Victim of domestic violence. - An individual against whom domestic violence, as described in G.S. 50B-1, has been committed.

(11)   Victim of a sexual offense. - An individual against whom a sexual offense, as described in Article 7A of Chapter 14 of the General Statutes, has been committed.

(12)   Victim of stalking. - An individual against whom stalking, as described in former G.S. 14-277.3 for acts occurring before December 1, 2008, or G.S. 14-277.3A for acts occurring on or after December 1, 2008, has been committed.

(13)   Victim of human trafficking. - An individual against whom human trafficking, as described in G.S. 14-43.11, has been committed. (2002-171, s. 1; 2007-547, s. 5; 2009-58, s. 4.)

§ 15C-3. Address Confidentiality Program.

The General Assembly establishes the Address Confidentiality Program in the Office of the Attorney General to protect the confidentiality of the address of a relocated victim of domestic violence, sexual offense, stalking, or human trafficking to prevent the victim's assailants or potential assailants from finding the victim through public records. Under this Program, the Attorney General shall designate a substitute address for a program participant and act as the agent of the program participant for purposes of service of process and receiving and forwarding first-class mail or certified or registered mail. The Attorney General shall not be required to forward any mail other than first-class mail or certified or registered mail to the program participant. The Attorney General shall not be required to track or otherwise maintain records of any mail received on behalf of a program participant unless the mail is certified or registered mail. (2002-171, s. 1; 2007-547, s. 6.)

§ 15C-4. Filing and certification of applications; authorization card.

(a)   An individual who wants to participate in the Address Confidentiality Program shall file an application with the Attorney General with the assistance of an application assistant. Any of the following individuals may apply to the Attorney General to have an address designated by the Attorney General to serve as the substitute address of the individual:

(1)   An adult individual.

(2)   A parent or guardian acting on behalf of a minor when the minor resides with the individual.

(3)   A guardian acting on behalf of an incapacitated individual.

(b)   The application shall be dated, signed, and verified by the applicant and shall be signed by the application assistant who assisted in the preparation of the application.

(c)   The application shall contain all of the following:

(1)   A statement by the applicant that the applicant is a victim of domestic violence, sexual offense, stalking, or human trafficking and that the applicant fears for the applicant's safety or the safety of the applicant's child.

(2)   Evidence that the applicant is a victim of domestic violence, sexual offense, stalking, or human trafficking. This evidence may include any of the following:

a.   Law enforcement, court, or other federal or state agency records or files.

b.   Documentation from a domestic violence program if the applicant is alleged to be a victim of domestic violence.

c.   Documentation from a religious, medical, or other professional from whom the applicant has sought assistance in dealing with the alleged domestic violence, sexual offense, or stalking.

d.   Documentation submitted to support a victim of human trafficking's application for federal assistance or benefits under federal human trafficking laws.

(3)   A statement by the applicant that disclosure of the applicant's address would endanger the applicant's safety or the safety of the applicant's child.

(4)   A statement by the applicant that the applicant has or will confidentially relocate in North Carolina.

(5)   A designation of the Attorney General as an agent for the applicant for purposes of service of process and the receipt of first-class mail or certified or registered mail.

(6)   The mailing address and telephone number where the applicant can be contacted by the Attorney General.

(7)   The address that the applicant requests not to be disclosed by the Attorney General that directly relates to the increased risk of domestic violence, sexual offense, or stalking.

(8)   A statement as to whether there is any existing court order or court action involving the applicant related to divorce proceedings, child support, child custody, or child visitation and the court that issued the order or has jurisdiction over the action.

(9)   A statement by the applicant that to the best of the applicant's knowledge, the information contained in the application is true.

(10)   A recommendation of an application assistant that the applicant have an address designated by the Attorney General to serve as the substitute address of the applicant.

(d)   Upon the filing of a properly completed application, the Attorney General shall certify the applicant as a program participant. Upon certification, the Attorney General shall issue an Address Confidentiality Program authorization card to the program participant. The Address Confidentiality Program

119

authorization card shall remain valid for so long as the program participant remains certified under the Program.

(e)   Applicants shall be certified for four years following the date of filing unless the certification is withdrawn or canceled prior to the end of the four-year period. A program participant may withdraw the certification by filing a request for withdrawal acknowledged before a notary with the Attorney General. A certification may be renewed by filing an application containing the information required by G.S. 15C-3 with the Attorney General at least 30 days prior to expiration of the current certification. (2002-171, s. 1; 2007-547, s. 7.)

§ 15C-5. Change of name, address, or telephone number.

(a)   A program participant shall notify the Attorney General within 30 days after the program participant has obtained a legal name change by providing the Attorney General a certified copy of any judgment or order evidencing the change or any other documentation the Attorney General deems to be sufficient evidence of the name change. If the program participant fails to notify the Attorney General of a name change in the manner provided in this subsection, the Attorney General shall cancel the certification of the program participant in the Program.

(b)   A program participant shall notify the Attorney General of a change in address or telephone number from the address or telephone number listed for the program participant on the application at least seven days before the change occurs. If the program participant fails to notify the Attorney General of a change in address or telephone number in the manner provided in this subsection, the Attorney General shall cancel the certification of the program participant in the Program. (2002-171, s. 1.)

§ 15C-6. Falsifying application information.

An applicant who falsely attests in an application that disclosure of the applicant's address would endanger the applicant's safety or the safety of the applicant's child or who knowingly provides false information when applying for certification or renewal shall lose certification in the Program. The Attorney General shall investigate violations of this section. Upon finding that a violation has occurred, the Attorney General shall assess a civil penalty against the applicant not to exceed five hundred dollars ($500.00). (2002-171, s. 1.)

§ 15C-7. Certification cancellation; records.

(a)   The Attorney General shall cancel the certification of a program participant under any of the following circumstances:

(1)   The program participant files a request for withdrawal of the certification pursuant to G.S. 15C-4.

(2)   The program participant fails to notify the Attorney General of a change in the program participant's name, address, or telephone number listed on the application pursuant to G.S. 15C-5.

(3)   The program participant submitted false information in applying for certification to the Program in violation of G.S. 15C-6.

(4)   Mail forwarded to the program participant by the Attorney General is returned as undeliverable.

(b)   The provisions of Article 3 of Chapter 150B of the General Statutes shall not apply to any cancellation of certification by the Attorney General pursuant to subsection (a) of this section.

(c)   The Attorney General shall send notice of cancellation to the program participant. Notice of cancellation shall set out the reasons for cancellation. The program participant shall have 30 days to appeal the cancellation decision under procedures developed by the Attorney General.

(d)   Any records or documents pertaining to a program participant shall be maintained in accordance with The General Schedule for State Agencies as established by the Department of Cultural Resources.

(e)   An individual who ceases to be a program participant is responsible for notifying persons who use the substitute address designated by the Attorney General as the program participant's address that the designated substitute address is no longer the individual's address. (2002-171, s. 1.)

§ 15C-8. Address use by State or local agencies.

(a)   The program participant, and not the Attorney General, is responsible for requesting that agencies of North Carolina use the address designated by the Attorney General as the substitute address of the program participant.

(b)   Except as otherwise provided in this section, when a program participant submits a current and valid Address Confidentiality Program authorization card to an agency of North Carolina, the agency shall accept the address designation by the Attorney General on the authorization card as the program participant's substitute address when creating a new public record.

(c)   An agency may request a waiver from the requirements of the Address Confidentiality Program by submitting a waiver request to the Attorney General. The agency's waiver request shall be in writing and include an explanation of why the agency cannot meet its statutory or administrative obligations by possessing or using the substitute address and an affirmation that, if the Attorney General accepts the waiver, the agency will only use the program participant's actual address for those statutory or administrative purposes.

(d)   The Attorney General's acceptance or denial of an agency's waiver request shall be made in writing and include a statement of specific reasons for acceptance or denial. Acceptance or denial of an agency's waiver request is not subject to further review.

(e)   A board of elections shall use the actual address of a program participant for all election-related purposes and shall keep the address confidential from the public under the provisions of G.S. 163-82.10(d). Use of the actual address on letters placed in the United States mail by a board of elections shall not be considered a breach of confidentiality. The substitute address designation provided by the Attorney General shall not be used as an address for voter registration or verification purposes.

(f)   For purposes of levying and collecting property taxes on motor vehicles pursuant to Article 22A of Chapter 105 of the General Statutes, the Attorney General shall issue to the county, city, or town assessor or tax collector a list containing the names and actual addresses of program participants residing in that county, city, or town. This list shall be used only for the purposes of listing, appraising, or assessing taxes on motor vehicles and collecting property taxes on motor vehicles in the county, city, or town. The county, city, or town assessor or tax collector or any current or former officer, employee, or agent of any

122

county, city, or town, who in the course of service to or employment by the county, city, or town has access to the name and actual address of a program participant, shall not disclose this information to any other person.

(g)   The substitute address designated by the Attorney General shall not be used for purposes of listing, appraising, or assessing taxes on property and collecting taxes on property under the provisions of Subchapter II of Chapter 105 of the General Statutes.

(h)   The substitute address designated by the Attorney General shall not be used as an address by any register of deeds on recorded documents or for the purpose of indexing land registered under Article 4 of Chapter 43 of the General Statutes in the index of registered instruments pursuant to G.S. 161-22.

(i)   A local school administrative unit shall use the actual address of a program participant for any purpose related to admission or assignment pursuant to Article 25 of Chapter 115C of the General Statutes and shall keep the actual address confidential from the public under the provisions of this Article. The substitute address designated by the Attorney General shall not be used as an address for admission or assignment purposes. For purposes of student records created under Chapter 115C of the General Statutes, the substitute address designated by the Attorney General shall be used.

(j)   Except as otherwise provided in this section, a program participant's actual address and telephone number maintained by an agency of North Carolina is not a public record within the meaning of Chapter 132 of the General Statutes. A program participant's actual address or telephone number maintained by the Attorney General or disclosed by the Attorney General pursuant to this Chapter is not a public record within the meaning of Chapter 132 of the General Statutes. (2002-171, s. 1.)

§ 15C-9. Disclosure of address prohibited.

(a)   The Attorney General is prohibited from disclosing any address or telephone number of a program participant other than the substitute address designated by the Attorney General, except under the following circumstances:

(1)   The information is requested by a federal, state, or local law enforcement agency for official use only.

(2)   The information is required by direction of a court order. However, any person to whom a program participant's address or telephone number has been disclosed shall not disclose the address or telephone number to any other person unless permitted to do so by order of the court.

(3)   Upon request by an agency to verify the participation of a specific program participant when the verification is for official use only.

(4)   Upon request by an agency, in the manner provided for by G.S. 15C-8.

(5)   The program participant is required to disclose the program participant's actual address as part of a registration required by Article 27A of Chapter 14 of the General Statutes.

(b)   The Attorney General shall provide immediate notification of disclosure to a program participant when disclosure is made pursuant to subdivision (2) or (4) of subsection (a) of this section.

(c)   If, at the time of application, an applicant is subject to a court order related to divorce proceedings, child support, child custody, or child visitation, the Attorney General shall notify the court that issued the order of the certification of the program participant in the Address Confidentiality Program and the substitute address designated by the Attorney General. If, at the time of application, an applicant is involved in a court action related to divorce proceedings, child support, child custody, or child visitation, the Attorney General shall notify the court having jurisdiction over the action of the certification of the applicant in the Address Confidentiality Program and the substitute address designated by the Attorney General.

(d)   No person shall knowingly and intentionally obtain a program participant's actual address or telephone number from the Attorney General or an agency knowing that the person is not authorized to obtain the address information.

(e)   No employee of the Attorney General or an agency shall knowingly and intentionally disclose a program participant's actual address or telephone number to a person known to the employee to be prohibited from receiving the program participant's actual address or telephone number, unless the disclosure is permissible by law. This subsection only applies when an employee obtains a program participant's actual address or telephone number during the course of the employee's official duties and, at the time of disclosure, the employee has

124

specific knowledge that the actual address or telephone number disclosed belongs to a program participant.

(f)   Any person who knowingly and intentionally obtains or discloses information in violation of this Chapter shall be guilty of a Class 1 misdemeanor and assessed a fine not to exceed two thousand five hundred dollars ($2,500). (2002-171, s. 1.)

§ 15C-10. Assistance for program applicants.

(a)   The Attorney General shall designate agencies of North Carolina and nonprofit organizations that provide counseling and shelter services to victims of domestic violence, sexual offense, stalking, or human trafficking to assist individuals applying to be program participants. Any assistance and counseling rendered by the Office of the Attorney General or its designee to applicants shall in no way be construed as legal advice.

(b)   The Attorney General, upon receiving notification pursuant to G.S. 15A-832(h), shall, within 96 hours of receiving the notification, issue the victim a letter of certification of eligibility or other relevant document entitling the person to have access to State benefits and services. (2002-171, s. 1; 2007-547, s. 8.)

§ 15C-11. Limited liability.

The State, agencies of North Carolina, and their officers, officials, employees, and agents, both past and present, in their official and individual capacities, shall be immune and held harmless from any liability in any action brought by or on behalf of any person injured or harmed by the actions or inactions of these entities and individuals in implementing this Chapter. However, if an employee's actions resulting in harm were not within the course and scope of the employee's duties, then that employee may be subject to suit as an individual to the extent permitted by the laws of the State of North Carolina. (2002-159, s. 28.5; 2002-171, s. 1.)

§ 15C-12. Rule-making authority.

The Attorney General is authorized to adopt any rules deemed necessary to carry out the provisions of this Chapter. (2002-171, s. 1.)

§ 15C-13. Additional time for action.

Whenever the laws of this State provide a program participant a legal right to act within a prescribed period of 10 days or less after the service of a notice or other paper upon the program participant, and the notice or paper is served upon the program participant by mail pursuant to this Chapter, five days shall be added to the prescribed

Chapter 16.

Gaming Contracts and Futures.

Article 1.

Gaming Contracts.

§ 16-1. Gaming and betting contracts void.

All wagers, bets or stakes made to depend upon any race, or upon any gaming by lot or chance, or upon any lot, chance, casualty or unknown or contingent event whatever, shall be unlawful; and all contracts, judgments, conveyances and assurances for and on account of any money or property, or thing in action, so wagered, bet or staked, or to repay, or to secure any money, or property, or thing in action, lent or advanced for the purpose of such wagering, betting, or staking as aforesaid, shall be void. (1810, c. 796, P.R.; R.C., c. 51, ss. 1, 2; Code, ss. 2841, 2842; Rev., s. 1687; C.S., s. 2142.)

§ 16-2. Players and betters competent witnesses.

No person shall be excused or incapacitated from confessing or testifying touching any money or property, or thing in action, so wagered, bet or staked, or lent for such purpose, by reason of his having won, played, bet or staked upon any game, lot or chance, casualty, or unknown or contingent event aforesaid;

but the confession or testimony of such person shall not be used against him, in any criminal prosecution, on account of such betting, wagering or staking. (R.C., c. 51, s. 3; Code, s. 2843; Rev., s. 1688; C.S., s. 2143.)

Article 2.

Contracts for "Futures."

§ 16-3. Certain contracts as to "futures" void.

Every contract, whether in writing or not, whereby any person shall agree to sell and deliver any cotton, Indian corn, wheat, rye, oats, tobacco, meal, lard, bacon, salt pork, salt fish, beef, cattle, sugar, coffee, stocks, bonds, and chooses in action, at a place and at a time specified and agreed upon therein, to any other person, whether the person to whom such article is so agreed to be sold and delivered shall be a party to such contract or not, when, in fact, and notwithstanding the terms expressed of such contract, it is not intended by the parties thereto that the articles or things so agreed to be sold and delivered shall be actually delivered, or the value thereof paid, but it is intended and understood by them that money or other thing of value shall be paid to the one party by the other, or to a third party, the party to whom such payment of money or other thing of value shall be made to depend, and the amount of such money or other thing of value so to be paid to depend upon whether the market price or value of the article so agreed to be sold and delivered is greater or less at the time and place so specified than the price stipulated to be paid and received for the articles so to be sold and delivered, and every contract commonly called "futures" as to the several articles and things hereinbefore specified, or any of them, by whatever other name called, and every contract as to the said several articles and things, or any of them, whereby the parties thereto contemplate and intend no real transaction as to the article or thing agreed to be delivered, but only the payment of a sum of money or other thing of value, such payment and the amount thereof and the person to whom the same is to be paid to depend on whether or not the market price or value is greater or less than the price so agreed to be paid for the said article or thing at the time and place specified in such contract, shall be utterly null and void; and no action shall be maintained in any court to enforce any such contract, whether the same was made in or out of the State, or partly in and partly out of this State, and whether made by the parties thereto by themselves or by or through their agents, immediately or mediately; nor shall any party to any such contract, or any agent of any such party, directly or remotely connected with any such contract in any way whatever, have or maintain any action or cause of action on account of any money or other thing of value paid or advanced or hypothecated by him or them in connection with or on account of such contract and agency; nor shall the courts of this State have any jurisdiction to entertain any suit or action brought upon a judgment based upon any such contract. This section shall not be construed so as to apply to any person, firm or corporation, or his or their agents, engaged in the business of manufacturing or wholesale merchandising in the purchase and/or sale of the necessary commodities required in the ordinary course of their business; nor shall this section be construed so as to apply to any contract with respect to the purchase and/or sale for future delivery of any of the articles or things mentioned and referred to in this section, where such purchase and/or sale is made on any exchange on which any such article or things are regularly bought and sold, or contracts therefor regularly entered into, and the rules and regulations of such exchange are such that either party to such contract may require delivery thereof: Provided, such contract is made in accordance with such rules and regulations.

In addition, this Article shall not apply to any person, firm, corporation, or other entity, either as principal or agent, or to any contract, that is excluded or exempted under the Commodity Exchange Act, as provided in section 16(e)(2) of the Commodity Exchange Act, 7 U.S.C. § 16(e)(2), and, accordingly, each section of this Article shall be considered a "law that regulates or prohibits the operation of bucket shops" within the meaning of section 16(e)(2) of the Commodity Exchange Act. (1889, c. 221, s. 1; 1905, c. 538, s. 7; Rev., s. 1689; 1909, c. 853, s. 1; C.S., s. 2144; 1931, c. 236, s. 1; 2001-110, s. 1.)

§ 16-4. Entering into or aiding contract for "futures" misdemeanor.

If any person shall become a party to any contract declared void in this Article; or if any person shall be the agent, directly or indirectly, of any party in making or furthering or effectuating the same; or if any agent or officer of a corporation shall in any manner knowingly aid in making or furthering any such contract to which the corporation is a party, he shall be guilty of a Class 1 misdemeanor.

If any person shall, while in this State, consent to become a party to any such contract made in another state, and if any person shall, as agent of any person or corporation, become a party to any such contract made in another state, or in this State do any act or in any way aid in the making or furthering of any such contract so made in another state, he shall be guilty of a Class 1 misdemeanor. (1889, c. 221, ss. 3, 4; Rev., ss. 3823, 3824; C.S., s. 2147; 1993, c. 539, s. 304; 1994, Ex. Sess., c. 24, s. 14(c).)

§ 16-5. Opening office for sales of "futures" misdemeanor.

If any person, corporation or other association of persons, either as principal or agent, shall establish or open an office or place of business in this State for the purpose of carrying on or engaging in making such contracts as are forbidden in this Article, he shall be guilty of a Class 1 misdemeanor. (1905, c. 538, ss. 1, 2; Rev., s. 3825; C.S., s. 2148; 1993, c. 539, s. 305; 1994, Ex. Sess., c. 24, s. 14(c).)

§ 16-6. Evidence in prosecutions under this Article.

No person shall be excused on any prosecution under the provisions of this Article from testifying touching anything done by himself or others contrary to the provisions thereof, but no discovery made by the witness upon such examination shall be used against him in any penal or criminal prosecution, and he shall be altogether pardoned of the offense so done or participated in by him. In all such prosecutions proof that the defendant was a party to a contract, as agent or principal, to sell and deliver any article, thing or property specified or named in this Article, or that he was the agent, directly or indirectly, of any party in making, furthering or effectuating the same, or that he was the agent or officer of any corporation or association or person in making, furthering or effectuating the same, and that the article, thing or property agreed to be sold and delivered was not actually delivered, and that settlement was made or agreed to be made upon the difference in value of said article, thing or property, shall constitute against such defendant prima facie evidence of guilt. Proof that any person, corporation or other association of persons, either as principal or agent, has established an office or place where are posted or published from information received the fluctuating prices of grain, cotton, provisions, stocks, bonds and other commodities, or of any one or more of the same, shall constitute prima facie evidence of being guilty of violating the provisions of this Article. (1905, c. 538, ss. 3, 4, 5; Rev., s. 3826; C.S., s. 2149.)

Chapter 17.

Habeas Corpus.

Article 1.

Constitutional Provisions.

§ 17-1. Remedy without delay for restraint of liberty.

Every person restrained of his liberty is entitled to a remedy to inquire into the lawfulness thereof, and to remove the same, if unlawful; and such remedy ought not to be denied or delayed. (Const., art. 1, s. 18; Rev., s. 1819; C.S., s. 2203.)

§ 17-2. Habeas corpus not to be suspended.

The privileges of the writ of habeas corpus shall not be suspended. (Const., art. 1, s. 21; Rev., s. 1820; C.S., s. 2204.)

Article 2.

Application.

§ 17-3. Who may prosecute writ.

Every person imprisoned or restrained of his liberty within this State, for any criminal or supposed criminal matter, or on any pretense whatsoever, except in cases specified in G.S. 17-4, may prosecute a writ of habeas corpus, according to the provisions of this Chapter, to inquire into the cause of such imprisonment or restraint, and, if illegal, to be delivered therefrom. (1868-9, c. 116, s. 1; Code, s. 1623; Rev., s. 1821; C.S., s. 2205.)

§ 17-4. When application denied.

Application to prosecute the writ shall be denied in the following cases:

130

(1)   Where the persons are committed or detained by virtue of process issued by a court of the United States, or a judge thereof, in cases where such courts or judges have exclusive jurisdiction under the laws of the United States, or have acquired exclusive jurisdiction by the commencement of suits in such courts.

(2)   Where persons are committed or detained by virtue of the final order, judgment or decree of a competent tribunal of civil or criminal jurisdiction, or by virtue of an execution issued upon such final order, judgment or decree.

(3)   Where any person has willfully neglected, for the space of two whole sessions after his imprisonment, to apply for the writ to the superior court of the county in which he may be imprisoned, such person shall not have a habeas corpus in vacation time for his enlargement.

(4)   Where no probable ground for relief is shown in the application. (1868-9, c. 116, s. 2; Code, s. 1624; Rev., s. 1822; C.S., s. 2206; 1971, c. 528, s. 1.)

§ 17-5. By whom application is made.

Application for the writ may be made either by the party for whose relief it is intended or by any person in his behalf. (1868-9, c. 116, s. 3; Code, s. 1625; Rev., s. 1823; C.S., s. 2207.)

§ 17-6. To judge of appellate division or superior court in writing.

Application for the writ shall be made in writing, signed by the applicant -

(1)   To any one of the justices or judges of the appellate division.

(2)   To any one of the superior court judges, either during a session or in vacation. (1868-9, c. 116, s. 4; Code, s. 1626; Rev., s. 1824; C.S., s. 2208; 1969, c. 44, s. 41; 1971, c. 528, s. 2.)

§ 17-7. Contents of application.

131

The application must state, in substance, as follows:

(1)   That the party, in whose behalf the writ is applied for, is imprisoned or restrained of his liberty, the place where, and the officer or person by whom he is imprisoned or restrained, naming both parties, if their names are known, or describing them if they are not known.

(2)   The cause or pretense of such imprisonment or restraint, according to the knowledge or belief of the applicant.

(3)   If the imprisonment is by virtue of any warrant or other process, a copy thereof shall be annexed, or it shall be made to appear that a copy thereof has been demanded and refused, or that for some sufficient reason a demand for such copy could not be made.

(4)   If the imprisonment or restraint is alleged to be illegal, the application must state in what the alleged illegality consists; and that the legality of the imprisonment or restraint has not been already adjudged, upon a prior writ of habeas corpus, to the knowledge or belief of the applicant.

(5)   The facts set forth in the application must be verified by the oath of the applicant, or by that of some other credible witness, which oath may be administered by any person authorized by law to take affidavits. (1868-9, c. 116, s. 5; Code, s. 1627; Rev., s. 1825; C.S., s. 2209.)

§ 17-8. Issuance of writ without application.

When the appellate division or superior court division, or any judge of either division, has evidence from any judicial proceeding before such court or judge that any person within this State is illegally imprisoned or restrained of his liberty, it is the duty of said court or judge to issue a writ of habeas corpus for his relief, although no application be made for such writ. (1868-9, c. 116, s. 10; Code, s. 1632; Rev., s. 1826; C.S., s. 2210; 1969, c. 44, s. 42.)

Article 3.

Writ.

§ 17-9. Writ granted without delay.

Any court or judge empowered to grant the writ, to whom such applications may be presented, shall grant the writ without delay, unless it appear from the application itself or from the documents annexed that the person applying or for whose benefit it is intended is, by this Chapter, prohibited from prosecuting the writ. (1868-9, c. 116, s. 6; Code, s. 1628; Rev., s. 1827; C.S., s. 2211.)

§ 17-10. Penalty for refusal to grant.

If any judge authorized by this Chapter to grant writs of habeas corpus refuses to grant such writ when legally applied for, every such judge shall forfeit to the party aggrieved two thousand five hundred dollars ($2,500). (1868-9, c. 116, s. 9; Code, s. 1631; Rev., s. 1828; C.S., s. 2212.)

§ 17-11. Sufficiency of writ; defects of form immaterial.

No writ of habeas corpus shall be disobeyed on account of any defect of form. It shall be sufficient -

(1)   If the person having the custody of the party imprisoned or restrained be designated either by his name of office, if he have any, or by his own name, or, if both such names be unknown or uncertain, he may be described by an assumed appellation, and anyone who may be served with the writ shall be deemed the person to whom it is directed, although it may be directed to him by a wrong name, or description, or to another person.

(2)   If the person who is directed to be produced be designated by name, or if his name be uncertain or unknown, he may be described by an assumed appellation or in any other way, so as to designate the person intended. (1868-9, c. 116, ss. 7, 8; Code, ss. 1629, 1630; Rev., s. 1829; C.S., s. 2213.)

§ 17-12. Service of writ.

The writ of habeas corpus may be served by any qualified elector of this State thereto authorized by the court or judge allowing the same. It may be served by delivering the writ, or a copy thereof, to the person to whom it is directed; or, if such person cannot be found, by leaving it, or a copy, at the jail, or other place in which the party for whose relief it is intended is confined, with some under officer or other person of proper age; or, if none such can be found, or if the person attempting to serve the writ be refused admittance, by affixing a copy thereof in some conspicuous place on the outside, either of the dwelling house of the party to whom the writ is directed or of the place where the party is confined for whose relief it is sued out. (1868-9, c. 116, s. 32; Code, s. 1657; Rev., s. 1833; C.S., s. 2214.)

Article 4.

Return.

§ 17-13. When writ returnable.

Writs of habeas corpus may be made returnable at a certain time, or forthwith, as the case may require. If the writ be returnable at a certain time, such return shall be made and the party shall be produced at the time and place specified therein. (1868-9, c. 116, s. 31; Code, s. 1656; Rev., s. 1830; C.S., s. 2215.)

§ 17-14. Contents of return; verification.

The person or officer on whom the writ is served must make a return thereto in writing, and, except where such person is a sworn public officer and makes his return in his official capacity, it must be verified by his oath. The return must state plainly and unequivocally -

(1)   Whether he has or has not the party in his custody or under his power or restraint.

(2)   If he has the party in his custody or power, or under his restraint, the authority and the cause of such imprisonment or restraint, setting forth the same at large.

134

(3)   If the party is detained by virtue of any writ, warrant, or other written authority, a copy thereof shall be annexed to the return; and the original shall be produced and exhibited on the return of the writ to the court or judge before whom the same is returnable.

(4)   If the person or officer upon whom such writ is served has had the party in his power or custody, or under his restraint, at any time prior or subsequent to the date of the writ, but has transferred such custody or restraint to another, the return shall state particularly to whom, at what time, for what cause and by what authority such transfer took place. (1868-9, c. 116, s. 11; Code, s. 1633; Rev., s. 1831; C.S., s. 2216.)

§ 17-15. Production of body if required.

If the writ requires it, the officer or person on whom the same has been served shall also produce the body of the party in his custody or power, according to the command of the writ, except in the case of the sickness of such party, as hereinafter provided. (1868-9, c. 116, s. 14; Code, s. 1636; Rev., s. 1832; C.S., s. 2217.)

Article 5.

Enforcement of Writ.

§ 17-16. Attachment for failure to obey.

If the person or officer on whom any writ of habeas corpus has been duly served refuses or neglects to obey the same, by producing the body of the party named or described therein, and by making a full and explicit return thereto, within the time required, and no sufficient excuse is shown for such refusal or neglect, it is the duty of the court or judge before whom the writ has been made returnable, upon due proof of the service thereof, forthwith to issue an attachment against such person or officer, directed to the sheriff of any county within this State, and commanding him forthwith to apprehend such person or officer and bring him immediately before such court or judge. On being so brought such person or officer shall be committed to close custody in the jail of the county where such court or judge may be, without being allowed the liberties thereof, until such

135

person or officer make return to such writ and comply with any order that may be made by such court or judge in relation to the party for whose relief the writ has been issued. (1868-9, c. 116, s. 15; Code, s. 1637; Rev., s. 1834; C.S., s. 2218.)

§ 17-17. Liability of judge refusing attachment.

If any judge willfully refuses to grant the writ of attachment, as provided for in G.S. 17-16, he shall be liable to impeachment, and moreover shall forfeit to the party aggrieved twenty-five hundred dollars ($2,500). (1870-1, c. 221, s. 2; Code, s. 1638; Rev., s. 1835; C.S., s. 2219.)

§ 17-18. Attachment against sheriff to be directed to coroner; procedure.

If a sheriff has neglected to return the writ agreeably to the command thereof, the attachment against him may be directed to the coroner or to any other person to be designated therein, who shall have power to execute the same, and such sheriff, upon being brought up, may be committed to the jail of any county other than his own. (1868-9, c. 116, s. 16; Code, s. 1639; Rev., s. 1836; C.S., s. 2220.)

§ 17-19. Precept to bring up party detained.

The court or judge by whom any such attachment may be issued may also at the same time, or afterwards, direct a precept to any sheriff, coroner, or other person to be designated therein, commanding him to bring forthwith before such court or judge the party, wherever to be found, for whose benefit the writ of habeas corpus has been granted. (1868-9, c. 116, s. 17; Code, s. 1640; Rev., s. 1837; C.S., s. 2221.)

§ 17-20. Liability of judge refusing precept.

If any judge refuses to grant the precept provided for in G.S. 17-19, he shall be liable to impeachment, and moreover shall forfeit to the party aggrieved twenty-five hundred dollars ($2,500). (1870-1, c. 221, s. 3; Code, s. 1641; Rev., s. 1838; C.S., s. 2222.)

§ 17-21. Liability of judge conniving at insufficient return.

If any judge grants the attachment, or the precept, and gives the officer or other person charged with the execution of the same verbal or written instructions not to execute the same, or to make any evasive or insufficient return, or any return other than that provided by law; or shall connive at the failing to make any return or any evasive or insufficient return, or any return other than that provided by law, he shall be liable to impeachment, and moreover shall forfeit to the party aggrieved twenty-five hundred dollars ($2,500). (1870-1, c. 221, s. 4; Code, s. 1642; Rev., s. 1839; C.S., s. 2223.)

§ 17-22. Power of county to aid service.

In the execution of any such attachment, precept or writ, the sheriff, coroner, or other person to whom it may be directed, may call to his aid the power of the county, as in other cases. (1868-9, c. 116, s. 18; Code, s. 1643; Rev., s. 1840; C.S., s. 2224.)

§ 17-23. Obedience to order of discharge compelled.

Obedience to a judgment or order for the discharge of a prisoner or person restrained of his liberty, pursuant to the provisions of this Chapter, may be enforced by the court or judge by attachment in the same manner and with the same effect as for a neglect to make return to a writ of habeas corpus; and the person found guilty of such disobedience shall forfeit to the party aggrieved two thousand five hundred dollars ($2,500), besides any special damages which such party may have sustained. (1868-9, c. 116, s. 24; Code, s. 1649; Rev., s. 1841; C.S., s. 2225.)

§ 17-24. No civil liability for obedience.

No officer or other person shall be liable to any civil action for obeying a judgment or order of discharge upon writ of habeas corpus. (1868-9, c. 116, s. 25; Code, s. 1650; Rev., s. 1842; C.S., s. 2226.)

§ 17-25. Recommittal after discharge; penalty.

If any person shall knowingly again imprison or detain one who has been set at large upon any writ of habeas corpus, for the same cause, other than by the legal process or order of the court wherein he is bound by recognizance to appear, or of any other court having jurisdiction in the case, he shall be guilty of a Class 1 misdemeanor. (1868-9, c. 116, s. 26; Code, s. 1651; Rev., s. 3581; C.S., s. 2227; 1993, c. 539, s. 306; 1994, Ex. Sess., c. 24, s. 14(c).)

§ 17-26. Disobedience to writ or refusing copy of process; penalty.

If any person to whom a writ of habeas corpus is directed shall neglect or refuse to make due return thereto, or to bring the body of the party detained according to the command of the writ without delay, or shall not, within six hours after demand made therefor, deliver a copy of the commitment or cause of detainer, such person shall, upon conviction on indictment, be fined one thousand dollars ($1,000), or imprisoned not exceeding 12 months, and if such person be an officer, shall moreover be removed from office. (1868-9, c. 116, s. 27; Code, s. 1652; Rev., s. 3597; C.S., s. 2228.)

§ 17-27. Penalty for false return.

If any person shall make a false return to a writ of habeas corpus, he shall be guilty of a Class 1 misdemeanor. (1868-9, c. 116, s. 28; Code, s. 1653; Rev., s. 3582; C.S., s. 2229; 1993, c. 539, s. 307; 1994, Ex. Sess., c. 24, s. 14(c).)

§ 17-28. Penalty for concealing party entitled to writ.

If anyone having in his custody, or under his power, any party who, by law, would be entitled to a writ of habeas corpus, or for whose relief such writ shall have been issued, shall, with intent to elude the service of such writ, or to avoid the effect thereof, transfer the party to the custody, or put him under the power or control, of another, or shall conceal or change the place of his confinement, or shall knowingly aid or abet another in so doing, he shall be guilty of a Class 1 misdemeanor. (1868-9, c. 116, ss. 29, 30; Code, ss. 1654, 1655; Rev., s. 3583; C.S., s. 2230; 1993, c. 539, s. 308; 1994, Ex. Sess., c. 24, s. 14(c).)

Article 6.

Proceedings and Judgment.

§ 17-29. Notice to interested parties.

When it appears from the return to the writ that the party named therein is in custody on any process, or by reason of any claim of right, under which any other person has an interest in continuing his imprisonment or restraint, no order shall be made for his discharge until it appears that the person so interested, or his attorney, if he have one, has had reasonable notice of the time and place at which such writ is returnable. (1868-9, c. 116, s. 12; 1870-1, c. 221, s. 1; Code, s. 1634; Rev., s. 1843; C.S., s. 2231.)

§ 17-30. Notice to district attorney.

When it appears from the return that such party is detained upon any criminal accusation, the court or judge may, if he thinks proper, make no order for the discharge of such party until sufficient notice of the time and place at which the writ has been returned, or is made returnable, is given to the district attorney of the district in which the person prosecuting the writ is detained. (1868-9, c. 116, s. 13; Code, s. 1635; Rev., s. 1844; C.S., s. 2232; 1973, c. 47, s. 2.)

§ 17-31. Subpoenas to witnesses.

Any party to a proceeding on a writ of habeas corpus may procure the attendance of witnesses at the hearing, by subpoena, to be issued by the clerk of any superior court, under the same rules, regulations and penalties prescribed by law in other cases. (1868-9, c. 116, s. 34; Code, s. 1659; Rev., s. 1845; C.S., s. 2233.)

§ 17-32. Proceedings on return; facts examined; summary hearing of issues.

The court or judge before whom the party is brought on a writ of habeas corpus shall, immediately after the return thereof, examine into the facts contained in such return, and into the cause of the confinement or restraint of such party, whether the same has been upon commitment for any criminal or supposed criminal matter or not; and if issue be taken upon the material facts in the return, or other facts are alleged to show that the imprisonment or detention is illegal, or that the party imprisoned is entitled to his discharge, the court or judge shall proceed, in a summary way, to hear the allegations and proofs on both sides, and to do what to justice appertains in delivering, bailing or remanding such party. (1868-9, c. 116, s. 19; Code, s. 1644; Rev., s. 1846; C.S., s. 2234.)

§ 17-33. When party discharged.

If no legal cause is shown for such imprisonment or restraint, or for the continuance thereof, the court or judge shall discharge the party from the custody or restraint under which he is held. But if it appears on the return to the writ that the party is in custody by virtue of civil process from any court legally constituted, or issued by any officer in the course of judicial proceedings before him, authorized by law, such party can be discharged only in one of the following cases:

(1)   Where the jurisdiction of such court or officer has been exceeded, either as to matter, place, sum or person.

(2)   Where, though the original imprisonment was lawful, yet by some act, omission or event, which has taken place afterwards, the party has become entitled to be discharged.

140

(3)   Where the process is defective in some matter of substance required by law, rendering such process void.

(4)   Where the process, though in proper form, has been issued in a case not allowed by law.

(5)   Where the person, having the custody of the party under such process, is not the person empowered by law to detain him.

(6)   Where the process is not authorized by any judgment, order or decree of any court, nor by any provision of law. (1868-9, c. 116, s. 20; Code, s. 1645; Rev., s. 1847; C.S., s. 2235.)

§ 17-34. When party remanded.

It is the duty of the court or judge forthwith to remand the party, if it appears that he is detained in custody, either -

(1)   By virtue of process issued by any court or judge of the United States, in a case where such court or judge has exclusive jurisdiction.

(2)   By virtue of the final judgment or decree of any competent court of civil or criminal jurisdiction, or of any execution issued upon such judgment or decree.

(3)   For any contempt specially and plainly charged in the commitment by some court, officer or body having authority to commit for the contempt so charged.

(4)   That the time during which such party may be legally detained has not expired. (1868-9, c. 116, s. 21; Code, s. 1646; Rev., s. 1848; C.S., s. 2236.)

§ 17-35. When the party bailed or remanded.

If it appears that the party has been legally committed for any criminal offense, or if it appears by the testimony offered with the return of the writ, or upon the hearing thereof, that the party is guilty of such an offense, although the

141

commitment is irregular, the court or judge shall proceed to let such party to bail, if the case is bailable and good bail is offered; if not, the court or judge shall forthwith remand such party to the custody or place him under the restraint from which he was taken, if the person or officer, under whose custody or restraint he was, is legally entitled thereto; if not so entitled, the court or judge shall commit such party to the custody of the officer or person legally entitled thereto. (1868-9, c. 116, s. 22; Code, s. 1647; Rev., s. 1849; C.S., s. 2237.)

§ 17-36. Party held in execution not to be discharged.

When a writ of habeas corpus cum causa issues and the sheriff or other officer to whom it is directed returns upon the same that the prisoner is condemned, by judgment given against him, and held in custody by virtue of an execution issued against him, the prisoner shall not be let to bail but shall be presently remanded, where he shall remain until discharged in due course of law. (2 Hen. V, c. 2; R.C., c. 31, s. 111; Code, s. 937; Rev., s. 1850; C.S., s. 2238.)

§ 17-37. When party ill, cause determined in his absence.

When, from the illness or infirmity of the person directed to be produced by a writ of habeas corpus, such person cannot, without danger, be brought before the court or judge where the writ is made returnable, the party in whose custody he is may state the fact in his return to the writ; and if the court or judge is satisfied of the truth of the allegation, and the return is otherwise sufficient, the court or judge shall proceed to decide on such return and to dispose of the matter in the same manner as if the body had been produced. (1868-9, c. 116, s. 23; Code, s. 1648; Rev., s. 1851; C.S., s. 2239.)

§ 17-38. No second committal after discharge; penalty.

No person who has been set at large upon any writ of habeas corpus shall be again imprisoned or detained for the same cause by any person whatsoever other than by the legal order or process of the court wherein he shall be bound by recognizance to appear or of any other court having jurisdiction in the case, under the penalty of two thousand five hundred dollars ($2,500) to the party aggrieved thereby. (1868-9, c. 116, s. 26; Code, s. 1651; Rev., s. 1852; C.S., s. 2240.)

Article 7.

Habeas Corpus for Custody of Children in Certain Cases.

§§ 17-39 through 17-40. Repealed by Session Laws 1967, c. 1153, s. 1.

Article 8.

Habeas Corpus Ad Testificandum.

§ 17-41. Authority to issue the writ.

Every court of record has power, upon the application of any party to any suit or proceeding, civil or criminal, pending in such court, to issue a writ of habeas corpus, for the purpose of bringing before the said court any prisoner who may be detained in any jail or prison within the State, for any cause, except a prisoner under sentence for a capital felony, to be examined as a witness in such suit or proceeding in behalf of the party making the application.

Such writ of habeas corpus may be issued by any magistrate or clerk of the superior court, upon application as provided in this section, to bring any person confined in the jail or prison of the same county where such magistrate or clerk may reside, to be examined as a witness before such magistrate or clerk.

In cases where the testimony of any prisoner is needed in a proceeding before a magistrate, or a clerk, and such person is confined in a county in which such magistrate or clerk does not reside, application for habeas corpus to testify may be made to any justice or judge of the General Court of Justice. (1868-9, c. 116, ss. 37, 38; Code, ss. 1663, 1664; Rev., ss. 1855, 1856; C.S., s. 2243; 1969, c. 44, s. 43; 1971, c. 528, s. 3.)

§ 17-42. Contents of application.

The application for the writ shall be made by the party to the suit or proceeding in which the writ is required, or by his agent or attorney. It must be verified by the applicant; and shall state-

(1)   The title and nature of the suit or proceeding in regard to which the testimony of such prisoner is desired.

(2)   That the testimony of such prisoner is material and necessary to such party on the trial or hearing of such suit or proceeding, as he is advised by counsel and verily believes. (1868-9, c. 116, s. 39; Code, s. 1665; Rev., s. 1857; C.S., s. 2244.)

§ 17-43. Service of writ.

The writ of habeas corpus to testify shall be served by the same person, and in like manner in all respects, and enforced by the court or officer issuing the same as prescribed in this Chapter for the service and enforcement of the writ of habeas corpus cum causa. (1868-9, c. 116, s. 40; Code, s. 1666; Rev., s. 1858; C.S., s. 2245.)

§ 17-44. Applicant to pay expenses and give bond to return.

The service of the writ shall not be complete, however, unless the applicant for the same tenders to the person in whose custody the prisoner may be, if such person is a sheriff, coroner, or marshal, the fees and expenses allowed by law for bringing such prisoner, nor unless he also gives bond, with sufficient security, to such sheriff, coroner, or marshal, as the case may be, conditioned that such applicant will pay the charges of carrying back such prisoner. (1868-9, c. 116, s. 41; Code, s. 1667; Rev., s. 1859; C.S., s. 2246; 1971, c. 528, s. 4.)

§ 17-45. Duty of officer to whom writ delivered or on whom served.

It is the duty of the officer to whom the writ is delivered or upon whom it is served, whether such writ is directed to him or not, upon payment or tender of the charges allowed by law, and the delivery or tender of the bond herein prescribed, to obey and return such writ according to the exigency thereof upon pain, on refusal or neglect, to forfeit to the party on whose application the same has been issued the sum of five hundred dollars ($500.00). (1868-9, c. 116, s. 42; Code, s. 1668; Rev., s. 1860; C.S., s. 2247.)

§ 17-46. Prisoner to be remanded.

After having testified, the prisoner shall be remanded to the prison from which he was taken. (1868-9, c. 116, s. 43; Code, s. 1669; Rev., s. 1861; C.S., s. 2248.)

Chapter 17A.

Law-Enforcement Officers.

§§ 17A-1 through 17A-9. Recodified as §§ 17C-1 through 17C-12.

Chapter 17B.

North Carolina Criminal Justice Education and Training System.

§§ 17B-1 through 17B-6. Recodified as §§ 17D-1 through 17D-4.

Chapter 17C.

North Carolina Criminal Justice Education and Training Standards Commission.

§ 17C-1. Findings and policy.

The General Assembly finds that the administration of criminal justice is of statewide concern, and that proper administration is important to the health, safety and welfare of the people of the State and is of such nature as to require education and training of a professional nature. It is in the public interest that such education and training be made available to persons who seek to become criminal justice officers, persons who are serving as such officers in a temporary or probationary capacity, and persons already in regular service. (1971, c. 963, s. 1; 1979, c. 763, s. 1.)

§ 17C-2. Definitions.

Unless the context clearly otherwise requires, the following definitions apply in this Chapter:

(1)   Commission. - The North Carolina Criminal Justice Education and Training Standards Commission.

(2)   Criminal justice agencies. - The State and local law-enforcement agencies, the State correctional agencies, other correctional agencies maintained by local governments, and the juvenile justice agencies, but shall not include deputy sheriffs, special deputy sheriffs, sheriffs' jailers, or other sheriffs' department personnel governed by the provisions of Chapter 17E of these General Statutes.

(3)   Criminal justice officers. - The administrative and subordinate personnel of all the departments, agencies, units or entities comprising the criminal justice agencies who are sworn law-enforcement officers, both State and local, with the power of arrest; State correctional officers; State probation/parole officers; State probation/parole officers-surveillance; officers, supervisory and administrative personnel of local confinement facilities; State juvenile justice officers; chief court counselors; and juvenile court counselors.

(4)   Entry level. - The initial appointment or employment of any person by a criminal justice agency, or any appointment or employment of a person previously employed by a criminal justice agency who has not been employed by a criminal justice agency for the 12-month period preceding this appointment or employment, or any appointment or employment of a previously certified criminal justice officer to a position which requires a different type of certification. (1971, c. 963, s. 2; 1979, c. 763, s. 1; 1983, c. 558, s. 2; c. 745, s. 2; 1989, c. 757, s. 1; 1989 (Reg. Sess., 1990), c. 1024, s. 4(a); 1997-503, s. 2; 2001-490, s. 1.1.)

§ 17C-3. North Carolina Criminal Justice Education and Training Standards Commission established; members; terms; vacancies.

(a)   There is established the North Carolina Criminal Justice Education and Training Standards Commission, hereinafter called "the Commission." The Commission shall be composed of 31 members as follows:

(1)   Police Chiefs. - Three police chiefs selected by the North Carolina Association of Chiefs of Police and one police chief appointed by the Governor.

(2)   Police Officers. - Three police officials appointed by the North Carolina Police Executives Association and two criminal justice officers certified by the Commission as selected by the North Carolina Law-Enforcement Officers' Association.

(3)   Departments. - The Attorney General of the State of North Carolina; the Secretary of Public Safety; the President of the North Carolina Community Colleges System.

(3a)   Repealed by Session Laws 2001-490, s. 1.2, effective June 30, 2001.

(4)   At-large Groups. - One individual representing and appointed by each of the following organizations: one mayor selected by the League of Municipalities; one law-enforcement training officer selected by the North Carolina Law-Enforcement Training Officers' Association; one criminal justice professional selected by the North Carolina Criminal Justice Association; one sworn law-enforcement officer selected by the North State Law-Enforcement Officers' Association; one member selected by the North Carolina Law-Enforcement Women's Association; and one District Attorney selected by the North Carolina Association of District Attorneys.

(5)   Citizens and Others. - The President of The University of North Carolina; the Dean of the School of Government at the University of North Carolina at Chapel Hill; and two citizens, one of whom shall be selected by the Governor and one of whom shall be selected by the Attorney General. The General Assembly shall appoint four persons, two upon the recommendation of the Speaker of the House of Representatives and two upon the recommendation of the President Pro Tempore of the Senate. Appointments by the General Assembly shall be made in accordance with G.S. 120-122. Appointments by the General Assembly shall be for two-year terms to conclude on June 30th in odd-numbered years.

147

(6)   Correctional Officers. - Four correctional officers in management positions employed by the Division of Adult Correction of the Department of Public Safety shall be appointed, two from the Section of Community Corrections of the Division of Adult Correction upon the recommendation of the Speaker of the House of Representatives and two from the Section of Prisons of the Division of Adult Correction upon the recommendation of the President Pro Tempore of the Senate. Appointments by the General Assembly shall be made in accordance with G.S. 120-122. Appointments by the General Assembly shall serve two-year terms to conclude on June 30th in odd-numbered years. The Governor shall appoint one correctional officer employed by the Division of Adult Correction of the Department of Public Safety and assigned to the Office of Staff Development and Training. The Governor's appointment shall serve a three-year term.

(b)   The members shall be appointed for staggered terms. The initial appointments shall be made prior to September 1, 1983, and the appointees shall hold office until July 1 of the year in which their respective terms expire and until their successors are appointed and qualified as provided hereafter:

For the terms of one year: one member from subdivision (1) of subsection (a) of this section, serving as a police chief; three members from subdivision (2) of subsection (a) of this section, one serving as a police official, and two criminal justice officers; one member from subdivision (4) of subsection (a) of this section, appointed by the North Carolina Law-Enforcement Training Officers' Association; and two members from subdivision (5) of subsection (a) of this section, one appointed by the Governor and one appointed by the Attorney General.

For the terms of two years: one member from subdivision (1) of subsection (a) of this section, serving as a police chief; one member from subdivision (2) of subsection (a) of this section, serving as a police official; and two members from subdivision (4) of subsection (a) of this section, one appointed by the League of Municipalities and one appointed by the North Carolina Association of District Attorneys.

For the terms of three years: two members from subdivision (1) of subsection (a) of this section, one police chief appointed by the North Carolina Association of Chiefs of Police and one police chief appointed by the Governor; one member from subdivision (2) of subsection (a) of this section, serving as a police official; and three members from subdivision (4) of subsection (a) of this section, one appointed by the North Carolina Law-Enforcement Women's Association, one

148

appointed by the North Carolina Criminal Justice Association, and one appointed by the North State Law-Enforcement Officers' Association.

Thereafter, as the term of each member expires, his successor shall be appointed for a term of three years. Notwithstanding the appointments for a term of years, each member shall serve at the will of the appointing authority.

The Attorney General, the President of The University of North Carolina, the Dean of the School of Government at the University of North Carolina at Chapel Hill, the President of the North Carolina Community Colleges System, and the Secretary of Public Safety shall be continuing members of the Commission during their tenure. These members of the Commission shall serve ex officio and shall perform their duties on the Commission in addition to the other duties of their offices. The ex officio members may elect to serve personally at any or all meetings of the Commission or may designate, in writing, one member of their respective office, department, university or agency to represent and vote for them on the Commission at all meetings the ex officio members are unable to attend.

Vacancies in the Commission occurring for any reason shall be filled, for the unexpired term, by the authority making the original appointment of the person causing the vacancy. A vacancy may be created by removal of a Commission member by majority vote of the Commission for misconduct, incompetence, or neglect of duty. A Commission member may be removed only pursuant to a hearing, after notice, at which the member subject to removal has an opportunity to be heard. (1971, c. 963, s. 3; 1977, c. 70, ss. 29, 30; 1979, c. 763, s. 1; 1981 (Reg. Sess., 1982), c. 1191, s. 31; 1983, c. 558, s. 3; c. 618, ss. 1, 2; c. 807, ss. 1, 2; 1987, c. 282, s. 4; 1989, c. 757, s. 2; 1995, c. 490, s. 15; 1997-443, s. 11A.118(a); 1998-202, s. 4(c); 2000-137, s. 4(d); 2000-140, s. 38.1(a); 2001-487, s. 5; 2001-490, s. 1.2; 2006-264, s. 29(c), (d); 2011-145, s. 19.1(g)-(k), (m); 2012-83, s. 29.)

§ 17C-4. Compensation.

(a)   Members of the Commission who are State officers or employees shall receive no compensation for serving on the Commission, but may be reimbursed for their expenses in accordance with G.S. 138-6. Members of the Commission who are full-time salaried public officers or employees other than State officers or employees shall receive no compensation for serving on the

Commission, but may be reimbursed for their expenses in accordance with G.S. 138-5(b). All other members of the Commission may receive compensation and reimbursement for expenses in accordance with G.S. 138-5.

(b)   The Chairman of the Commission may appoint such ad hoc members of the Commission's standing and select committees as are necessary to carry out the business of the Commission, and such service shall be reimbursed as provided in G.S. 17C-4(a), subject to the approval of the Attorney General. (1971, c. 963, s. 4; 1979, c. 763, s. 1; 1989, c. 757, s. 3.)

§ 17C-5. Chairman; vice-chairman; other officers; meetings; reports.

(a)   The Commission shall elect one of the members of the Commission as Chairman at the first regular meeting after July 1 of each year. The ex officio members shall not be eligible for election as Chairman.

(b)   The Commission shall select a vice-chairman and such other officers and committee chairmen from among its members as it deems desirable at the first regular meeting of the Commission after its creation and at the first regular meeting after July 1 of each year thereafter. Nothing in this subsection, however, shall prevent the creation or abolition of committees or offices of the Commission, other than the office of vice-chairman, as the need may arise at any time during the year.

(c)   The Commission shall hold at least four regular meetings per year upon the call of the chairman. Special meetings shall be held upon the call of the chairman or the vice-chairman, or upon the written request of five members of the Commission. Such special meetings must be held within 30 days.

(d)   The Commission shall present regular and special reports and recommendations to the Attorney General or the General Assembly, or both, as the need may arise or as the Attorney General or General Assembly may request. (1971, c. 963, s. 5; 1979, c. 763, s. 1; 1983, c. 807, s. 3.)

§ 17C-6. (See Editor's Note) Powers of Commission.

(a)   In addition to powers conferred upon the Commission elsewhere in this Chapter, the Commission shall have the following powers, which shall be enforceable through its rules and regulations, certification procedures, or the provisions of G.S. 17C-10:

(1)   Promulgate rules and regulations for the administration of this Chapter, which rules may require (i) the submission by any criminal justice agency of information with respect to the employment, education, retention, and training of its criminal justice officers, and (ii) the submission by any criminal justice training school of information with respect to its criminal justice training programs that are required by this Chapter.

(2)   Establish minimum educational and training standards that must be met in order to qualify for entry level employment and retention as a criminal justice officer in temporary or probationary status or in a permanent position. The standards for entry level employment shall include education and training in response to, and investigation of, domestic violence cases, as well as training in investigation for evidence-based prosecutions.

(3)   Certify and recertify, suspend, revoke, or deny, pursuant to the standards that it has established for the purpose, persons as qualified under the provisions of this Chapter to be employed at entry level and retained as criminal justice officers.

(4)   Establish minimum standards for the certification of criminal justice training schools and programs or courses of instruction that are required by this Chapter.

(5)   Certify and recertify, suspend, revoke, or deny, pursuant to the standards that it has established for the purpose, criminal justice training schools and programs or courses of instruction that are required by this Chapter.

(6)   Establish minimum standards and levels of education and experience for all criminal justice instructors and school directors who participate in programs or courses of instruction that are required by this Chapter.

(7)   Certify and recertify, suspend, revoke, or deny, pursuant to the standards that it has established for the purpose, criminal justice instructors and school directors who participate in programs or courses of instruction that are required by this Chapter.

(8)   Investigate and make such evaluations as may be necessary to determine if criminal justice agencies, schools, and individuals are complying with the provisions of this Chapter.

(9)   Adopt and amend bylaws, consistent with law, for its internal management and control.

(10)   Enter into contracts incident to the administration of its authority pursuant to this Chapter.

(11)   Establish minimum standards and levels of training for certification and periodic recertification of operators of and instructors for training programs in radio microwave, laser, and other electronic speed-measuring instruments.

(12)   Certify and recertify, suspend, revoke, or deny, pursuant to the standards that it has established, operators and instructors for training programs for each approved type of radio microwave, laser, and other electronic speed-measuring instruments.

(13)   In conjunction with the Secretary of Public Safety, approve use of specific models and types of radio microwave, laser, and other speed-measuring instruments and establish the procedures for operation of each approved instrument and standards for calibration and testing for accuracy of each approved instrument.

(13a)   Expired effective September 30, 2007. See note.

(14)   Establish minimum standards for in-service training for criminal justice officers. In-service training standards shall include training in response to, and investigation of, domestic violence cases, as well as training investigation for evidence-based prosecutions.

(15)   Establish minimum standards and levels of training for certification of instructors for the domestic violence training required by subdivisions (2) and (14) of this subsection.

(16)   Establish standards and guidelines for the annual firearms certification of qualified retired law enforcement officers, as defined in G.S. 14-415.10(4a), to efficiently implement the provisions of G.S. 14-415.25. The standards shall provide for the courses, qualifications, and the issuance of the annual firearms qualification certification. The Commission may adopt any rules necessary to

152

effect the provisions of this section, and may charge a reasonable fee to applicants for the costs incurred in compliance with this subdivision.

(b)   The Commission shall have the following powers, which shall be advisory in nature and for which the Commission is not authorized to undertake any enforcement actions:

(1)   Identify types of criminal justice positions, other than entry level positions, for which advanced or specialized training and education are appropriate, and establish minimum standards for the certification of persons as being qualified for those positions on the basis of specified education, training, and experience; provided, that compliance with these minimum standards shall be discretionary on the part of criminal justice agencies with respect to their criminal justice officers;

(2)   Certify, pursuant to the standards that it has established for the purpose, criminal justice officers for those criminal justice agencies that elect to comply with the minimum education, training, and experience standards established by the Commission for positions for which advanced or specialized training, education, and experience are appropriate;

(3)   Consult and cooperate with counties, municipalities, agencies of this State, other governmental agencies, and with universities, colleges, junior colleges, and other institutions concerning the development of criminal justice training schools and programs or courses of instruction;

(4)   Study and make reports and recommendations concerning criminal justice education and training in North Carolina;

(5)   Conduct and stimulate research by public and private agencies which shall be designed to improve education and training in the administration of criminal justice;

(6)   Study, obtain data, statistics, and information and make reports concerning the recruitment, selection, education, retention, and training of persons serving criminal justice agencies in this State; to make recommendations for improvement in methods of recruitment, selection, education, retention, and training of persons serving criminal justice agencies;

(7)   Make recommendations concerning any matters within its purview pursuant to this Chapter;

153

(8)   Appoint such advisory committees as it may deem necessary;

(9)   Do such things as may be necessary and incidental to the administration of its authority pursuant to this Chapter;

(10)   Formulate basic plans for and promote the development and improvement of a comprehensive system of education and training for the officers and employees of criminal justice agencies consistent with its rules and regulations;

(11)   Maintain liaison among local, State and federal agencies with respect to criminal justice education and training;

(12)   Promote the planning and development of a systematic career development program for criminal justice professionals.

(c)   All decisions and rules and regulations heretofore made by the North Carolina Criminal Justice Training and Standards Council and the North Carolina Criminal Justice Education and Training System Council shall remain in full force and effect unless and until repealed or suspended by action of the North Carolina Criminal Justice Education and Training Standards Commission established herein. The present Councils are terminated on December 31, 1979, and their power, duties and responsibilities vest in the North Carolina Criminal Justice Education and Training Standards Commission effective January 1, 1980.

(d)   The standards established by the Commission pursuant to G.S. 17C-6(a)(11) and 17C-6(a)(12) and by the Commission and the Secretary of Public Safety pursuant to G.S. 17C-6(a)(13) shall not be less stringent than standards established by the U.S. Department of Transportation, National Highway Traffic Safety Administration, National Bureau of Standards, or the Federal Communications Commission. (1971, c. 963, s. 6; 1975, c. 372, s. 2; 1979, c. 763, s. 1; 1979, 2nd Sess., c. 1184, ss. 1, 2; 1989, c. 757, s. 4; 1994, Ex. Sess., c. 18, s. 2; 1995, c. 509, s. 14.1; 2000-140, s. 38.1(b); 2002-159, s. 29; 2003-280, s. 3; 2004-186, ss. 2.1, 2.3, 2.5; 2005-27, ss. 1, 2; 2007-427, s. 2; 2009-546, s. 2; 2011-145, s. 19.1(g).)

§ 17C-7. Functions of the Department of Justice.

(a)   The Attorney General shall provide such staff assistance as the Commission shall require in the performance of its duties.

(b)   The Attorney General shall have legal custody of all books, papers, documents, or other records and property of the Commission.

(c)   Any papers, documents, or other records which become the property of the Commission that are placed in the criminal justice officer's personnel file maintained by the Commission shall be subject to the same disclosure requirements as set forth in Chapters 126, 153A, and 160A of the General Statutes regarding the privacy of personnel records. (1979, c. 763, s. 1; 1989, c. 757, s. 5.)

§ 17C-8. System established.

The North Carolina Criminal Justice Education and Training Standards Commission shall establish a North Carolina Criminal Justice Education and Training System. The system shall be a cooperative arrangement among criminal justice agencies, both State and local, and criminal justice education and training schools, both public and private, to provide education and training to the officers and employees of the criminal justice agencies of the State of North Carolina and its local governments. Members of the system shall include the North Carolina Justice Academy as well as such other public or private agencies or institutions within the State, that are engaged in criminal justice education and training, and desire to be affiliated with the system for the purpose of achieving greater coordination of criminal justice education and training efforts in North Carolina. (1979, c. 763, s. 1.)

§ 17C-9. Criminal Justice Standards Division of the Department of Justice established; appointment of director; duties.

(a)   There is hereby established, within the Department of Justice, the Criminal Justice Standards Division, hereinafter called "the Division," which shall be organized and staffed in accordance with applicable laws and regulations and within the limits of authorized appropriations.

(b)   The Attorney General shall appoint a director for the Division chosen from a list of three nominees submitted to him by the Commission who shall be responsible to and serve at the pleasure of the Attorney General and the Commission.

(c)   The Division shall administer such programs as are assigned to it by the Commission. The Division shall also administer such additional related programs as may be assigned to it by the Attorney General or the General Assembly. Administrative duties and responsibilities shall include, but are not limited to, the following:

(1)   Administering any and all programs assigned to the Division by the Commission and reporting any violations of or deviations from the rules and regulations of the Commission as the Commission may require;

(2)   Compiling data, developing reports, identifying needs and performing research relevant to beneficial improvement of the criminal justice agencies;

(3)   Developing new and revising existing programs for adoption consideration by the Commission;

(4)   Monitoring and evaluating programs of the Commission;

(5)   Providing technical assistance to relevant agencies of the criminal justice system to aid them in the discharge of program participation and responsibilities;

(6)   Disseminating information on Commission programs to concerned agencies and/or individuals;

(7)   Taking such other actions as may be deemed necessary or appropriate to carry out its assigned duties and responsibilities;

(8)   The director may divulge any information in the Division's personnel file of a criminal justice officer or applicant for certification to the head of the criminal justice agency employing the officer or considering the applicant for employment when the director deems it necessary and essential to the retention or employment of said officer or applicant. The information may be divulged whether or not such information was contained in a personnel file maintained by a State or by a local government agency. (1979, c. 763, s. 1; 1983, c. 807, s. 4.)

§ 17C-10. Required standards.

(a)   Criminal justice officers shall not be required to meet any requirement of subsections (b) and (c) of this section as a condition of continued employment, nor shall failure of any such criminal justice officer to fulfill such requirements make him ineligible for any promotional examination for which he is otherwise eligible if the criminal justice officer held a permanent appointment prior to June 1, 1986, and is an officer, supervisor or administrator of a local confinement facility; prior to March 15, 1973, and is a sworn law enforcement officer with power of arrest; prior to January 1, 1974, and is a State adult correctional officer; prior to July 1, 1975, and is a State probation/parole officer; prior to July 1, 1974, and is a State youth services officer; prior to January 15, 1980, and is a State probation/parole intake officer, prior to April 1, 1983, and is a State parole case analyst; prior to December 14, 1983, and is a State probation/parole officer-surveillance; or prior to February 1, 1987, and is a State probation/parole intensive officer.

The legislature finds, and it is declared to be the policy of this Chapter, that such criminal justice officers have satisfied such entry level requirements by their experience. It is the intent of the Chapter that all criminal justice officers employed at the entry level after the Commission has adopted the required standards shall meet the requirements of this Chapter. All criminal justice officers who are exempted from the required entry level standards by this subsection shall be subject thereafter to the requirements of subsections (b) and (c) of this section as well as the requirements of G.S. 17C-6(a) in order to retain certification.

If any criminal justice officer exempted from the required standards by this provision fails to serve as a criminal justice officer for a 12-month period, said officer shall be required to comply with the required entry level standards established by the Commission pursuant to the authority otherwise granted in this section and in G.S. 17C-6(a).

(b)   The Commission shall provide, by regulation, for a period of probationary employment and certification for criminal justice officers. The Commission may prescribe such training requirements as are required for the award of either probationary or permanent certification of officers, in addition to the pre-employment requirements authorized in G.S. 17C-6(a). Any criminal justice officer appointed on a temporary or probationary basis who does not comply with the training provisions of this Chapter is not authorized to exercise the powers of a criminal justice officer to include the power of arrest. If,

157

however, a criminal justice officer has enrolled in a Commission-approved preparatory program of training that concludes later than the end of the officer's probationary period, and the Commission does not require such training to be completed prior to the award of probationary certification, the Commission may extend, for good cause shown, the probationary period for a period not to exceed six months.

Upon separation of a criminal justice officer from a criminal justice agency within the prescribed period of temporary or probationary appointment, the officer's probationary certification shall be terminated by the Commission. Upon the reappointment to the same agency or appointment to another criminal justice agency of an officer who has separated from an agency within the probationary period, the officer shall be charged with the cumulative amount of time served during his initial or subsequent appointments and allowed the remainder of the probationary period to complete the Commission's requirements. Upon reappointment to the same agency or appointment to another agency of an officer who has separated from an agency within the probationary period and who has remained out of service for more than one year after the date of separation, the officer shall be allowed another probationary period to satisfy the Commission's requirements.

(c)   In addition to the requirements of subsection (b) of this section, the Commission, by rules and regulations, shall fix other qualifications for the employment, training, and retention of criminal justice officers including minimum age, education, physical and mental standards, citizenship, good moral character, experience, and such other matters as relate to the competence and reliability of persons to assume and discharge the responsibilities of criminal justice officers, and the Commission shall prescribe the means for presenting evidence of fulfillment of these requirements.

Where minimum educational standards are not met, yet the individual shows potential and a willingness to achieve the standards by extra study, they may be waived by the Commission for the reasonable amount of time it will take to achieve the standards required. Such an educational waiver shall not exceed 12 months.

(d)   The Commission may issue a certificate evidencing satisfaction of the requirements of subsections (b) and (c) of this section to any applicant who presents such evidence as may be required by its rules and regulations of satisfactory completion of a program or course of instruction in another jurisdiction equivalent in content and quality to that required by the Commission for approved criminal justice education and training programs in this State. (1971, c. 963, s. 1; 1979, c. 763, s. 1; 1981, c. 8; c. 400; 1983, c. 745, s. 3; 1989, c. 757, s. 6.)

§ 17C-11. Compliance; enforcement.

(a)   Any criminal justice officer who the Commission determines does not comply with this Chapter or any rules adopted under this Chapter shall not exercise the powers of a criminal justice officer and shall not exercise the power of arrest unless the Commission waives that certification or deficiency. The Commission shall enforce this section by the entry of appropriate orders effective upon service on either the criminal justice agency or the criminal justice officer.

(a1)   Any criminal justice training school, program, or course of instruction that the Commission determines does not comply with this Chapter, or any rules adopted under this Chapter, shall not continue to offer programs or courses of instruction unless the Commission waives that certification or deficiency. Any criminal justice instructor, school director, commission certified operator, and any commission certified instructor, who the Commission determines does not comply with this Chapter, or any rules adopted under this Chapter, shall not act as an instructor, school director, or operator unless the Commission waives that certification or deficiency. The Commission shall enforce this section by the entry of appropriate orders effective upon service on the criminal justice training school or the individual holding commission certification.

(b)   Any person who desires to appeal the proposed denial, suspension, or revocation of any certification authorized to be issued by the Commission shall file a written appeal with the Commission not later than 30 days following notice of denial, suspension, or revocation.

(c)   The Commission may appear in its own name and apply to courts having jurisdiction for injunctions to prevent violations of this Chapter or of rules issued pursuant thereto; specifically, the performance of criminal justice officer functions by officers or individuals who are not in compliance with the standards and requirements of G.S. 17C-6(a) and G.S. 17C-10. A single act of performance of a criminal justice officer function by an officer or individual who is performing such function in violation of this Chapter is sufficient, if shown, to invoke the injunctive relief of this section. (1979, c. 763, s. 1; 1989, c. 757, s. 7; 2001-490, s. 1.3; 2009-546, s. 3.)

§ 17C-12. Grants under the supervision of Commission and the State; donations and appropriations.

(a)   The Commission may accept for any of its purposes and functions under this Chapter any and all donations, both real and personal, and grants of money from any governmental unit or public agency, or from any institution, person, firm or corporation, and may receive, utilize and dispose of the same. Any arrangements pursuant to this section shall be detailed in an annual report of the Commission. Such report shall include the identity of the donor, the nature of the transaction, and the conditions, if any. Any money received by the Commission pursuant to this section shall be deposited in the State Treasury to the account of the Commission.

(b)   The Commission may authorize the reimbursement to each political subdivision of the State not exceeding sixty percent (60%) of the salary and of the allowable tuition, living and travel expenses incurred by the officers in attendance at approved training programs, providing said political subdivisions do in fact adhere to the selection and training standards established by the Commission.

(c)   The Commission by rules and regulations, shall provide for administration of the grant program authorized by this section. In promulgating such rules, the Commission shall promote the most efficient and economical program of criminal justice training, including the maximum utilization of existing facilities and programs for the purpose of avoiding duplication.

(d)   The Commission may provide grants as a reimbursement for actual expenses incurred by the State or political subdivision thereof for the provisions of training programs of officers from other jurisdictions within the State. (1971, c. 963, ss. 8, 9; 1979, c. 763, s. 1.)

§ 17C-13. Pardons; expunctions.

(a)   When a person presents competent evidence that he has been granted an unconditional pardon for a crime in this State, any other state, or the United States, the Commission may not deny, suspend, or revoke that person's certification based solely on the commission of that crime or for an alleged lack of good moral character due to the commission of that crime.

(b)   Notwithstanding G.S. 15A-145.4 or G.S. 15A-145.5, the Commission may gain access to a person's felony conviction records, including those maintained by the Administrative Office of the Courts in its confidential files containing the names of persons granted expunctions. The Commission may deny, suspend, or revoke a person's certification based solely on that person's felony conviction, whether or not that conviction was expunged. (1989, c. 757, s. 8; 2011-278, s. 3; 2012-191, s. 6.)

Chapter 17D.

North Carolina Justice Academy.

§ 17D-1. Definitions.

As used in this Chapter, unless the context otherwise requires:

(1)   "Academy" means the North Carolina Justice Academy.

(2)   "Academy property" means property that is owned or leased in whole or in part by the State of North Carolina and which is subject to the general management and control of the Department of Justice and is located in Salemburg, North Carolina, or at any other locations within the State which are dedicated to the use of the North Carolina Justice Academy subsequent to this Chapter being enacted.

(3)   "The Commission" means the North Carolina Criminal Justice Education and Training Standards Commission.

(4)   "Criminal justice agencies" means the State and local law enforcement agencies, the State and local police traffic service agencies, the State correctional agencies, the jails and other correctional agencies maintained by local governments, the courts of the State and the juvenile justice agencies.

(5)   "Criminal justice personnel" means any person who serves or assists any State or local agency engaged in crime prevention, crime reduction, crime investigation, training or educating of persons employed by criminal justice agencies, or enforcement of the criminal law; or any person employed by a criminal justice agency.

(6)   "Department" means the Department of Justice. (1973, c. 749; 1977, c. 831, s. 1; 1979, c. 763, s. 2; 1997-456, s. 27.)

§ 17D-2. Academy established; duties.

(a)   The North Carolina Department of Justice shall establish a North Carolina Justice Academy.

(b)   The Department of Justice shall employ the staff of the academy and direct its operations.

(c)   Duties of the academy. The North Carolina Justice Academy shall have, but is not limited to, the following functions:

(1)   It may provide training programs for criminal justice personnel.

(2)   It may provide technical assistance upon request to criminal justice agencies to aid them in the discharge of their responsibilities.

(3)   It may develop, publish, and distribute educational and training materials.

(4)   It may take such other actions as may be deemed necessary or appropriate to carry out its assigned duties and responsibilities. (1973, c. 749; 1979, c. 763, s. 2.)

§ 17D-3. Donations.

The Department of Justice may accept for any of its purposes and functions under this Article any and all donations, both real and personal, and grants of money from any governmental unit or public agency, or from any institution,

162

person, firm or corporation. Any arrangements pursuant to this section shall be detailed in an annual report of the academy. Such reports shall include the identity of the donor, the nature of the transaction, and the conditions, if any. Any money received by the Department of Justice pursuant to this section shall be deposited in the State Treasury to the account of the academy. All moneys involved shall be subject to audit by the State Auditor. (1979, c. 763, s. 2.)

§ 17D-4. Application of State highway and motor vehicles laws at the academy; authority of Department of Justice to regulate traffic, etc.

(a)   Except as otherwise provided in this section, all of the provisions of Chapter 20 of the General Statutes relating to the use of highways of the State and the operation of vehicles thereon are applicable to all streets, alleys, driveways, and parking lots on academy property. Nothing in this section modifies any rights of ownership or control of academy property, now or hereafter vested in the State of North Carolina ex rel., Department of Justice.

(b)   The Department of Justice may by ordinance prohibit, regulate, divert, control, and limit pedestrian or vehicular traffic and the parking of vehicles and other modes of conveyance on the campus. In fixing speed limits, the Department of Justice is not subject to G.S. 20-141(f) or (g), but may fix any speed limit reasonable and safe under the circumstances as conclusively determined by the Department of Justice. The Department of Justice may not regulate traffic on streets open to the public as of right, except as specifically provided in this section.

(c)   The Department of Justice may by ordinance provide for the registration of vehicles maintained or operated on the campus by any student, faculty member, or employee of the academy and may fix fees for such registration. The ordinance may make it unlawful for any person to operate an unregistered vehicle on the campus when the vehicle is required by the ordinance to be registered.

(d)   The Department of Justice may by ordinance set aside parking lots on the campus for use by students, faculty, and employees of the academy and members of the general public attending schools, conferences, or meetings at the academy, visiting or making use of any academy facilities, or attending to official business with the academy. The Department of Justice may issue permits to park in these lots and may charge a fee therefor. The Department of

163

Justice may also by ordinance make it unlawful for any person to park a vehicle in any lot or other parking facility without procuring the requisite permit and displaying it on the vehicle.

(e)   The Department of Justice may by ordinance provide for the issuance of stickers, decals, permits or other indicia representing the registration of vehicles or the eligibility of vehicles to park on the campus and may by ordinance prohibit the forgery, counterfeiting, unauthorized transfer, or unauthorized use of such stickers, decals, permits or other indicia.

(f)   Violation of an ordinance adopted under any portion of this section is a Class 3 misdemeanor. An ordinance may provide that certain acts prohibited thereby shall not be enforced by criminal sanctions, and in such cases a person committing any such act shall not be guilty of a misdemeanor.

(g)   An ordinance adopted under this section may provide that a violation will subject the offender to a civil penalty. Penalties may be graduated according to the seriousness of the offense or the number of prior offenses committed by the person charged. The Department of Justice may establish procedure for the collection of these penalties and may enforce the penalties by civil action in the nature of debt. The Department of Justice may also provide for appropriate administrative sanctions if an offender does not pay a validly due penalty or has committed repeated offenses. Appropriate administrative sanctions include, but are not limited to, revocation of parking permits, termination of vehicle registration, and termination or suspension of enrollment in or employment by the academy.

(h)   An ordinance adopted under this section may provide that any vehicle illegally parked may be removed to a storage area, in which case the person so removing the vehicle shall be deemed a legal possessor within the meaning of G.S. 44A-2(d).

(i)   Evidence that a vehicle was found parked or unattended in violation of a council ordinance is prima facie evidence that the vehicle was parked by:

(1)   The person holding an academy parking permit for the vehicle;

(2)   If no academy parking permit has been issued for the vehicle, the person in whose name the vehicle is registered with the academy pursuant to subsection (c); or

164

(3)   If no academy parking permit has been issued for the vehicle and the vehicle is not registered with the academy, the person in whose name it is registered with the North Carolina Department of Motor Vehicles or the corresponding agency of another state or nation.

The rule of evidence established by this subsection applies only in civil, criminal, or administrative actions or proceedings concerning violations of ordinances of the Department of Justice. G.S. 20-162.1 does not apply to such actions or proceedings.

(j)   The Department of Justice shall cause to be posted appropriate notice to the public of applicable traffic and parking restrictions.

(k)   All ordinances adopted under this section shall be filed in the offices of the North Carolina Attorney General and the Secretary of State. The Department of Justice shall provide for printing and distributing copies of its traffic and parking ordinances.

(l)   All moneys received pursuant to this section shall be State funds as defined in G.S. 143C-1-1. (1977, c. 831, s. 2; 1979, c. 763, s. 2; 1993, c. 539, s. 309; 1994, Ex. Sess., c. 24, s. 14(c); 2006-203

Chapter 17E.

North Carolina Sheriffs' Education and Training Standards Commission.

§ 17E-1. Findings and policy.

The General Assembly finds and declares that the office of sheriff, the office of deputy sheriff and the other officers and employees of the sheriff of a county are unique among all of the law-enforcement offices of North Carolina. The administration of criminal justice has been declared by Chapter 17C of the General Statutes to be of statewide concern to the people of the State. The sheriff is the only officer of local government required by the Constitution. The sheriff, in addition to his criminal justice responsibilities, is the only officer who is also responsible for the courts of the State, and acting as their bailiff and marshall. The sheriff administers and executes criminal and civil justice and acts as the ex officio detention officer.

The deputy sheriff has been held by the Supreme Court of this State to hold an office of special trust and confidence, acting in the name of and with powers coterminous with his principal, the elected sheriff.

The offices of sheriff and deputy sheriff are therefore of special concern to the public health, safety, welfare and morals of the people of the State. The training and educational needs of such officers therefore require particularized and differential treatment from those of the criminal justice officers certified under Chapter 17C of the General Statutes. (1983, c. 558, s. 1; 1995, c. 103, s. 1.)

§ 17E-2. Definitions.

Unless the context clearly requires otherwise, the following definitions apply to this Chapter:

(1)   "Commission" means the North Carolina Sheriffs' Education and Training Standards Commission.

(2)   "Office" or "department" means the sheriff of a county, his deputies, his employees and such equipment, space, provisions and quarters as are supplied for their use.

(3)   "Justice officer" means:

a.   A person who, through the special trust and confidence of the sheriff, has taken the oath of office prescribed by Chapter 11 of the General Statutes as a peace officer in the office of the sheriff. This term includes "deputy sheriffs", "reserve deputy sheriffs", and "special deputy sheriffs", but does not include clerical and support personnel not required to take an oath. The term "special deputy" means a person who, through appointment by the sheriff, becomes an unpaid criminal justice officer to perform a specific act directed by the sheriff; or

b.   A person who, through the special trust and confidence of the sheriff, has been appointed as a detention officer by the sheriff; or

c.   A person who is either the administrator or other custodial personnel of district confinement facilities as defined in G.S. 153A-219; however, nothing in this Chapter transfers any supervisory or administrative control over employees of district confinement facilities to the office of the sheriff; or

d.   A person who, through the special trust and confidence of the sheriff, is under the direct supervision and control of the sheriff and serves as a telecommunicator, or who is presented to the Commission for appointment as a telecommunicator by an employing entity other than the sheriff for the purpose of obtaining certification from the Commission as a telecommunicator. (1983, c. 558, s. 1; c. 745, s. 1; 1991, c. 265, s. 1; 1995, c. 103, s. 2; 1997-443, s. 20.11(b).)

§ 17E-3. North Carolina Sheriffs' Education and Training Standards Commission established; members; terms; vacancies.

(a)   There is hereby established the North Carolina Sheriffs' Education and Training Standards Commission. The Commission shall be composed of 17 members as follows:

(1)   Sheriffs. - Twelve sheriffs appointed by the North Carolina Sheriffs' Association, 10 representing each of the Commission Districts established in this section, and two appointed at large in such manner as shall be prescribed by the Constitution or bylaws of the Association.

(2)   Appointees of the General Assembly. - One person appointed by the Speaker of the House of Representatives pursuant to G.S. 120-121 and one person appointed by the General Assembly upon the recommendation of the President Pro Tempore of the Senate pursuant to G.S. 120-121.

(3)   County Commissioners. - One county commissioner appointed by the Governor as recommended from three nominees from the North Carolina Association of County Commissioners.

(4)   Others. - The President of the Community Colleges System or the President's designee and the Dean of the School of Government at the University of North Carolina at Chapel Hill or the Dean's designee shall be ex officio, nonvoting members of the Commission.

(b)   Terms. - Members shall be appointed for staggered terms. Beginning September 1, 1995, sheriffs representing Commission Districts 3, 6, and 9 shall be appointed to three-year terms; sheriffs representing Commission Districts 1, 4, and 7 shall be appointed to one-year terms; sheriffs representing Commission Districts 2, 5, 8, and 10 and the two at-large sheriffs, shall be appointed to two-year terms. The appointee of the House of Representatives shall serve a term of two years. The appointee of the Senate shall serve a term of two years. The county commissioner appointed by the North Carolina Association of County Commissioners shall serve a term of two years. After the initial terms established herein have expired, all sheriffs appointed to the Commission shall be appointed to terms of three years.

If an individual ceases to be a sheriff then his seat on the Commission becomes vacated upon his ceasing to be qualified to hold that seat. Any individual appointed or designated to serve on this Commission shall serve until his successor is appointed and qualified.

(c)   Vacancies. - If any vacancy occurs in the membership of the Commission, the appointing authority shall appoint another person to fill the unexpired term of the vacating member.

(d)   Compensation. - None of the members of the Commission shall receive compensation for serving on the Commission. However, if the North Carolina Department of Justice has funds available, then members of the Commission who are State officers or employees may be reimbursed for their expenses in accordance with G.S. 138-6; members of the Commission who are full-time salaried public officers or employees other than State officers or employees may be reimbursed for their expenses in accordance with G.S. 138-5(b). All other members of the Commission may receive compensation and reimbursement for expenses in accordance with G.S. 138-5.

(e)   Officers. - The chairman shall be elected from among the membership. The Commission shall select its other officers from among the membership as it deems necessary. All officers serve for one year, or until successors are qualified.

(f)   Removal. - The Commission may remove a member for misfeasance, malfeasance, nonfeasance or neglect of duty.

(g)   The Commission has power to adopt its own rules of procedure. The Commission shall meet no less than four times a year. It shall also meet on the call of the chairman or vice-chairman, or any four members of the Commission.

(h)   The Commission may appoint any resident of the State to an adjunct or special committee created or appointed by it to study or make recommendations or reports on any subject matter related to its duties or the office of sheriff.

(i)   Members of the Commission shall have the authority to designate, in writing, one member of his office to represent them and, if the member possesses voting authority, vote for them on the Commission at all meetings the voting member is unable to attend. This voting authority shall extend to all matters brought before the Commission which require a vote, to include the entry of final agency decisions and the adoption of administrative rules.

(j)   The State is divided into 10 Commission Districts established for the appointment of members of the North Carolina Sheriffs' Education and Training Standards Commission as follows:

District 1: The Counties of Bertie, Camden, Chowan, Currituck, Gates, Hertford, Pasquotank, Perquimans, Tyrrell, and Washington.

District 2: The Counties of Caswell, Edgecombe, Franklin, Granville, Halifax, Nash, Northampton, Person, Vance, and Warren.

District 3: The Counties of Beaufort, Craven, Dare, Duplin, Hyde, Jones, Lenoir, Martin, Pamlico, and Pitt.

District 4: The Counties of Chatham, Durham, Greene, Harnett, Johnston, Lee, Orange, Wake, Wayne, and Wilson.

District 5: The Counties of Alleghany, Alexander, Ashe, Catawba, Gaston, Lincoln, Surry, Watauga, Wilkes, and Yadkin.

District 6: The Counties of Alamance, Davidson, Davie, Forsyth, Guilford, Iredell, Randolph, Rockingham, Rowan, and Stokes.

District 7: The Counties of Bladen, Brunswick, Carteret, Columbus, Cumberland, New Hanover, Onslow, Pender, Robeson, and Sampson.

District 8: The Counties of Anson, Cabarrus, Hoke, Mecklenburg, Montgomery, Moore, Richmond, Scotland, Stanly, and Union.

District 9: The Counties of Avery, Burke, Caldwell, Cleveland, Madison, McDowell, Mitchell, Polk, Rutherford, and Yancey.

District 10: The Counties of Buncombe, Cherokee, Clay, Graham, Haywood, Henderson, Jackson, Macon, Swain, and Transylvania. (1983, c. 558, s. 1; 1991

(Reg. Sess., 1992), c. 1005, ss. 1, 2; 1993 (Reg. Sess., 1994), c. 562, s. 1; c. 767, s. 33; 1995, c. 103, s. 3; c. 490, s. 48; 2006-264, s. 29(e).)

§ 17E-4. Powers and duties of the Commission.

(a)   The Commission shall have the following powers, duties, and responsibilities, which are enforceable through its rules and regulations, certification procedures, or the provisions of G.S. 17E-8 and G.S. 17E-9:

(1)   Promulgate rules and regulations for the administration of this Chapter, which rules may require (i) the submission by any agency of information with respect to the employment, education, and training of its justice officers, and (ii) the submission by any training school of information with respect to its programs that are required by this Chapter;

(2)   Establish minimum educational and training standards that may be met in order to qualify for entry level employment as an officer in temporary or probationary status or in a permanent position. The standards for entry level employment of officers shall include training in response to, and investigation of, domestic violence cases, as well as training in investigation for evidence-based prosecutions. For purposes of the domestic violence training requirement, the term "officers" shall include justice officers as defined in G.S. 17E-2(3)a., except that the term shall not include "special deputy sheriffs" as defined in G.S. 17E-2(3)a.;

(3)   Certify, pursuant to the standards that it may establish for the purpose, persons as qualified under the provisions of this Chapter who may be employed at entry level as officers;

(4)   Establish minimum standards for the certification of training schools and programs or courses of instruction that are required by this Chapter;

(5)   Certify, pursuant to the standards that it has established for the purpose, training schools and programs or courses of instruction that are required by this Chapter;

(6)   Establish standards and levels of education or equivalent experience for teachers who participate in programs or courses of instruction that are required by this Chapter;

170

(7)   Certify, pursuant to the standards that it has established for the purpose, teachers who participate in programs or courses of instruction that are required by this Chapter;

(8)   Investigate and make such evaluations as may be necessary to determine if agencies are complying with the provision of this Chapter;

(9)   Adopt and amend bylaws, consistent with law, for its internal management and control;

(10)   Enter into contracts incident to the administration of its authority pursuant to this Chapter;

(11)   Establish minimum standards for in-service training for justice officers. In-service training standards shall include training in response to, and investigation of, domestic violence cases, as well as training in investigation for evidence-based prosecutions. For purposes of the domestic violence training requirement, the term "justice officer" shall include those defined in G.S. 17E-2(3)a., except that the term shall not include "special deputy sheriffs" as defined in G.S. 17E-2(3)a.;

(12)   Establish minimum standards and levels of training for certification of instructors for the domestic violence training required by subdivisions (2) and (11) of this subsection.

The Commission may certify, and no additional certification shall be required from it, programs, courses and teachers certified by the North Carolina Criminal Justice Education and Training Standards Commission. Where the Commission determines that a program, course, instructor or teacher is required for an area which is unique to the office of sheriff, the Commission may certify such program, course, instructor, or teacher under such standards and procedures as it may establish.

(b)   The Commission shall have the following powers, which shall be advisory in nature and for which the Commission is not authorized to undertake any enforcement actions:

(1)   Certify, pursuant to the standards that it has established for the purpose, justice officers for those law-enforcement agencies that elect to comply with the minimum education, training, and experience standards established by the

171

Commission for positions for which advanced or specialized training, education, and experience are appropriate;

(2)   Consult and cooperate with counties, agencies of this State, other governmental agencies, and with universities, colleges, junior colleges, and other institutions, public or private, concerning the development of training schools and programs or courses of instruction;

(3)   Study and make reports and recommendations concerning justice education and training in North Carolina;

(4)   Conduct and stimulate research by public and private agencies which shall be designed to improve education and training in the administration of justice;

(5)   Study, obtain data, statistics, and information and make reports concerning the recruitment, selection, education and training of persons serving justice agencies in this State; to make recommendations for improvement in methods of recruitment, selection, education and training of persons serving sheriffs' departments;

(6)   Study and make reports and recommendations to the Governor, Attorney General, Chief Justice, President of the Senate and Speaker of the House, concerning the manpower, salary and equipment needs of the sheriffs of the State;

(7)   Make recommendations concerning any matters within its purview pursuant to this Chapter;

(8)   Appoint such advisory committees as it may deem necessary;

(9)   Do such things as may be necessary and incidental to the administration of its authority pursuant to this Chapter;

(10)   Formulate basic plans for and promote the development and improvement of a comprehensive system of education and training for the officers and employees of agencies consistent with its rules and regulations;

(11)   Maintain liaison among municipal, State and federal agencies with respect to education and training;

172

(12)   Promote the planning and development of a systematic career development program for sheriffs' department personnel. (1983, c. 558, s. 1; 1991, c. 265, s. 2; 1995, c. 103, ss. 4, 5; 2004-186, ss. 2.7, 2.9, 2.10, 2.12.)

§ 17E-5. Functions of the Department of Justice.

(a)   The Attorney General shall provide such staff assistance as the Commission shall require and direct in the performance of its duties.

(b)   The Attorney General shall have legal custody of all books, papers, documents, or other records and property of the Commission. (1983, c. 558, s. 1.)

§ 17E-6. Justice Officers' Standards Division established; appointment of director; duties.

(a)   There is hereby established, within the Department of Justice, the Justice Officers' Standards Division hereinafter called "the Division," which shall be organized and staffed in accordance with applicable laws and regulations and within the limits of authorized appropriations.

(b)   The Attorney General shall appoint a director for the Division chosen from a list of nominees submitted to him by the Commission who shall be responsible to and serve at the pleasure of the Attorney General and the Commission.

(c)   The Division shall administer such programs as are assigned to it by the Commission. Administrative duties and responsibilities shall include, but are not limited to, the following:

(1)   Administering any and all programs assigned to the Division by the Commission and reporting any violations of or deviations from the rules and regulations of the Commission as the Commission may require;

(2)   Compiling data, developing reports, identifying needs and performing research relevant to improvement of the agencies;

173

(3)   Developing new and revising existing programs for adoption consideration by the Commission;

(4)   Monitoring and evaluating programs of the Commission;

(5)   Providing technical assistance to agencies of the justice system to aid them in the discharge of program participation and responsibilities;

(6)   Disseminating information on Commission programs to concerned agencies or individuals;

(7)   Taking such other actions as may be deemed necessary or appropriate to carry out its assigned duties and responsibilities;

(8)   The director may divulge any information in the Division's personnel file of a justice officer or applicant for certification to the head of the department employing the officer or considering the applicant for employment when the director deems it necessary and essential to the retention or employment of said officer or applicant. The information may be divulged whether or not such information was contained in a personnel file maintained by a State or by a local government agency. (1983, c. 558, s. 1; 1995, c. 103, s. 6.)

§ 17E-7. Required standards.

(a)   Justice officers, other than those set forth in subsection (c1) of this section, shall not be required to meet any requirements of subsections (b) and (c) of this section as a condition of continued employment, nor shall failure of a justice officer to fulfill such requirements make him ineligible for any promotional examination for which he is otherwise eligible if the officer held an appointment prior to July 1, 1983, and is a sworn law-enforcement officer with power of arrest. The legislature finds, and it is hereby declared to be the policy of this Chapter, that such officers have satisfied such requirements by their experience. It is the intent of the Chapter that all justice officers employed at the entry level after the Commission has adopted the required standards shall meet the requirements of this Chapter. All justice officers who are exempted from the required entry level standards by this subsection are subject to the requirements of subsections (b) and (c) of this section as well as the requirements of G.S. 17E-4(a) in order to retain certification.

174

(b)   The Commission shall provide, by regulation, that no person may be appointed as a justice officer at entry level, except on a temporary or probationary basis, unless such person has satisfactorily completed an initial preparatory program of training at a school certified by the Commission or has been exempted from that requirement by the Commission pursuant to this Chapter. Upon separation of a justice officer from a sheriff's department within the temporary or probationary period of appointment, the probationary certification shall be terminated by the Commission. Upon the reappointment to the same department or appointment to another department of an officer who has separated from a department within the probationary period, the officer shall be charged with the amount of time served during his initial appointment and allowed the remainder of the probationary period to complete the basic training requirement. Upon the reappointment to the same department or appointment to another department of an officer who has separated from a department within the probationary period and who has remained out of service for more than one year from the date of separation, the officer shall be allowed another probationary period to complete such training as the Commission shall require by rule for an officer returning to service.

(c)   In addition to the requirements of subsection (b) of this section, the Commission, by rules and regulations, may fix other qualifications for the employment and retention of justice officers including minimum age, education, physical and mental standards, citizenship, good moral character, experience, and such other matters as relate to the competence and reliability of persons to assume and discharge the responsibilities of the office, and the Commission shall prescribe the means for presenting evidence of fulfillment of these requirements.

Where minimum educational standards are not met, yet the individual shows potential and a willingness to achieve the standards by extra study, they may be waived by the Commission for the reasonable amount of time it will take to achieve the standards required. Upon petition from a sheriff, the Commission may grant a waiver of any provisions of this section (17E-7) for any justice officer serving that sheriff.

(c1)   Any justice officer appointed as a telecommunicator at the entry level after March 1, 1998, shall meet all requirements of this Chapter. Any person employed in the capacity of a telecommunicator as defined by the Commission on or before March 1, 1998, shall not be required to meet any entry-level requirements as a condition of continued employment but shall be reported to the Commission for certification. All justice officers who are exempted from the

175

required entry-level standards by this subsection are subject to the requirements of subsections (b) and (c) of this section as well as the requirements of G.S. 17E-4(a) in order to retain certification.

(d)   The Commission may issue a certificate evidencing satisfaction of the requirements of subsections (b), (c), and (c1) of this section to any applicant who presents such evidence as may be required by its rules and regulations of satisfactory completion of a program or course of instruction in another jurisdiction. (1983, c. 558, s. 1; 1987, c. 783, s. 8; 1991, c. 265, s. 3; 1995, c. 103, s. 7; 1997-443, s. 20.11(c).)

§ 17E-8. Special requirements; authorizations.

(a)   Nothing in this Chapter shall be construed as a condition precedent to the taking of the oath of office or the exercise of the powers, duties or privileges of the offices of sheriff or justice officer.

(b)   Any sheriff or justice officer, who has taken the oath of office, or person who has received a special deputation for the purpose from the sheriff, acts validly, and his arrests, executions, levies and sales are valid, without regard to whether he has complied with this Chapter or the rules or regulations adopted under this Chapter, unless he has been ordered to cease and desist from such actions by the court, or pursuant to G.S. 17E-9. (1983, c. 558, s. 1; 1995, c. 103, s. 8.)

§ 17E-9. Compliance; enforcement.

(a)   Any justice officer who the Commission determines does not comply with this Chapter or any rules adopted under this Chapter shall not exercise the powers of a justice officer and shall not exercise the power of arrest unless the Commission waives that certification or deficiency. The Commission shall enforce this section by the entry of appropriate orders effective upon service on either the department or the justice officer.

(b)   Any person who desires to appeal the proposed denial, suspension, or revocation of any certification authorized to be issued by the Commission shall file a written appeal with the Commission not later than 30 days following notice of denial, suspension, or revocation.

(c) The Commission may appear in its own name and apply to courts having jurisdiction for injunctions to prevent violations of this Chapter or of rules issued pursuant thereto; specifically, the performance of justice officer functions by officers or individuals who are not in compliance with the standards and requirements of this Chapter or of rules issued pursuant thereto. A single act of performance of a justice officer function by an officer or individual who is performing such function in violation of this Chapter is sufficient, if shown, to invoke the injunctive relief of this section. (1983, c. 558, s. 1; 1995, c. 103, s. 9; 2001-490, s. 1.4.)

§ 17E-10. Donations to the Commission; grants and appropriations.

(a) The Commission may accept for any of its purposes and functions under this Chapter any and all donations, both real and personal, and grants of money from any governmental unit or public agency, or from any institution, person, firm or corporation, and may receive, utilize and dispose of same. Any arrangement pursuant to this section shall be detailed in a biennial report of the Commission to the General Assembly. Such report shall include the identity of the donor, the nature of the transaction, and the conditions, if any. Any money received by the Commission pursuant to this section shall be deposited in the State Treasury to the account of the Commission.

(b) The Commission may authorize grants pursuant to this section and consistent with the powers conferred upon the Commission under G.S. 17E-6.

(c) The Commission in providing for the administration of the grant program authorized by this section shall promote the most efficient and economical program of criminal justice education and training, including the maximum utilization of existing facilities and programs for the purpose of avoiding duplication.

(d) The Commission may provide grants as a reimbursement for actual expenses incurred by the State or any political subdivision thereof for the provision of training programs providing said political subdivisions and State law-enforcement agencies do adhere to the selection and training standards established by the Commission. (1983, c. 558, s. 1; 1991 (Reg. Sess., 1992), c. 1030, s. 9.)

§ 17E-11. Application and construction of Chapter.

(a)   Nothing in this Chapter shall apply to the sheriff elected by the people.

(b)   Nothing in this Chapter shall be construed as modifying the character of a sheriff from an elective office, or as modifying the character of the office of deputy sheriff from an appointive office.

(c)   If a justice officer, or a criminal justice officer as defined in G.S. 17C-2(c), becomes sheriff, the justice officer is not required to maintain certification for the period served as sheriff. The Commission shall reinstate certification upon the conclusion of the period of service as sheriff and in conformance with the rules of the Commission for the application for certification. (1983, c. 558, s. 1; 1991, c. 265, s. 4.)

§ 17E-12. Pardons; expunctions.

(a)   When a person presents competent evidence that the person has been granted an unconditional pardon of innocence for a crime in this State, any other state, or the United States, the Commission may not deny, suspend, or revoke that person's certification based solely on the commission of that crime or for alleged lack of good moral character due to the commission of that crime.

(b)   Notwithstanding G.S. 15A-145.4 or G.S. 15A-145.5, the Commission may gain access to a person's felony conviction records, including those maintained by the Administrative Office of the Courts in its confidential files containing the names of persons granted expunctions. The Commission may deny, suspend, or revoke a person's certification based solely on that person's felony conviction, whether or not that conviction was expunged. (1995, c. 103, s. 10; 2011-278, s. 4; 2012-191, s. 7.)

Vision Books Order Form

Fax Orders:	1-980-299-5965
Phone Orders:	1-704-898-0770
E-mail Orders:	www.visionbooks.org
Mail Orders:	Vision Books, LLC P.O. Box 42406 Charlotte, NC 28215

Shipp To:
Name_____
Address_____
City_____State_____Zip_____
Phone_____Fax_____
Email_____@_____

Bill To: We can bill a third party on your behalf.
Name_____
Address_____
City_____State_____Zip_____
Phone____(_____)_____Fax_____
Email_____@_____

Pamphlet Number ($15.00 Each)	Qty	Total Cost
_____	_____	_____
_____	_____	_____
_____	_____	_____
_____	_____	_____
_____	_____	_____
_____	_____	_____
_____	_____	_____
_____	_____	_____
Full Volume Set 1-92	92 Pamphlets	1,380.00

Free Shipping Shipping & Handling on Full Volume Orders
Add $1.00 Shipping & Handling per pamphlet $_____

Total Cost $_____

Thank you for your support. Management!

DID YOU ENJOY THIS BOOK?

Vision Books would like to hear from you! If you or someone you know has been falsely imprisoned, we would like to hear your story. If the 'North Carolina Criminal Law and Procedure' has had an effect in your life or if you have suggestions, we would like to hear from you. Send your letters to:

Vision Books, LLC
Attn: Staff Writers
P.O. Box 42406
Charlotte, NC 28215
Email: staff@visionbooks.org

Order Additional Copies:

Fax Orders: 1-980-299-5965

Phone Orders: 1-704-898-0770
E-mail Orders: www.visionbooks.org

Mail Orders: Vision Books, LLC
                                 P.O. Box 42406
                                 Charlotte, NC 28215